ACTORS WORKING

The Actor's Guide to Marketing Success

by

Clair Sinnett

Georgia Publishing, USA

Actors Working™ – The Actor's Guide to Marketing Success

Published by:
Georgia Publishing, USA, an Imprint of Actors Working Books
531 Main Street, #1135, El Segundo, CA 90245
www.actorsworking.com

Sinnett, Clair
Actors Working™ – The Actor's Guide to Marketing Success/
Clair Sinnett.—1st ed.
p.   cm.
ISBN 0-9740573-4-7
1. xxxxx 2. xxxx I. Title
2003

Original book cover concept and design by Bradford Hill.
Edited by Candi Barthelemy. Final edit by Lisa Wysocky.
Typesetting, Layout, and Design by Lisa Wysocky (lisawysocky@comcast.net).

All photographs are used with the kind permission of the actors and/or photographers.
Pepsi, "Alonzo's" commercial: Script and storyboards reprinted with the kind permission of PepsiCo.
Brand: Pepsi-Cola, Agency: BBDO, New York
The 'Actors Working' sign logo is a trademark of Actors Working Books.

For general information on Actors Working products and/or a schedule for workshops taught by Clair Sinnett, please see our website, www.actorsworking.com or call (866) 4-ACTORS.

For information on licensing domestic rights, authorization to photocopy items for corporate, personal, or educational use, please call (866) 4-ACTORS.

For press review copies or for author interviews and other publicity information, please call (866) 4-ACTORS.

Cataloging-in-Publication Data for this book is available from the Library of Congress. 2003108980 PCN
Printed in the United States of America
1 3 5 7 9 10 8 6 4 2

This publication is designed to provide accurate and authoritative information in regard to the subject matter covered. It is sold with the understanding that the publisher is not engaged in rendering career counseling or other professional services. If expert assistance is required, the services of a competent professional person should be sought.

The Industry Speaks

"Very concise! This book is such a valuable tool for actors."
Linda Phillips-Palo, CSA, casting director

"Good, solid information. If you have ever said, 'What do I do now?'—this book is for you!"
Bruce Economou, manager – John Crosby Management

"Clair's reputation in the business as both a casting director and teacher is impressive. Naturally, those of us who are aware of her teaching skills and trust her taste would never turn down a chance to meet one of her students."
Judy Savage, agent – The Savage Agency

"I feel her students are some of the most prepared to enter the business and succeed."
Vaughn D. Hart, agent – Vaughn D. Hart & Associates

"Her insight in this business is invaluable! Clair single handedly helped me jump from Graduate school to one of the top ten agencies in the entertainment business."
Alan Mingo, Jr., 'Simba' – "The Lion King"

"She has a keen sense of what an actor needs to do to make it in this industry and stay there. Clair's marketing plan incorporates a successful step-by-step process that focuses exactly on what agents and casting directors are looking for in an actor."
Richard Padro, former student

"One of the few books on acting that will actually be helpful to the young artists."
Bobby Moresco, writer/director

"Thanks to Clair's approach, I booked three nationals and a few regional spots in my first year!"
Beth Malone, former student

"She is a positive influence on all she encounters. She encourages rather than discourages talent and helps the advancement of what's good in the artist as well as our industry."
Al Onorato, manager – Handprint Entertainment

"This is a must read for any serious actor starting their career."
Rodger Smith, Ph.D., acting option coordinator
Assoc. Professor, Dep't. of Theatre and Dance, Ball State University

"Many acting teachers teach you how to *act* the role, Clair teaches you how to *get* the role!!"
Daniel Hepner, former student

"Ms. Sinnett's enthusiasm for teaching promising young actors may only be surpassed by her desire to see them succeed."
Martin Weiss, manager – ETS Management

"Her gifts as a teacher are remarkable and renown in the industry."
Charles Matthau, producer/director – The Matthau Company

"Clair taught me how to . . . target . . . specific agents, managers, and casting directors that are looking for my type, what type of questions to ask, what type of questions to expect to answer, and what to do when I finally got my foot in the door . . . It's almost like getting the answer key before taking a test."
Swan Kim, former student

"I am convinced that I would be on that sinking boat had I not developed a strategic marketing plan (before I graduated) under the keen eye of Clair Sinnett. The crux of Clair's marketing program relies on her own words: "There is a reason why the term is 'Show Business' and not 'Show Art'.""
Will Jude, former student

"Clair's passion is contagious and energizes all she comes in contact with."
Keith Lewis, agent – The Morgan Agency

"She has a remarkable eye for talent and is an astounding teacher."
Neil Bagg, agent – Don Buchwald & Associates, Inc.

"Clair Sinnett's students always win top awards and sign with major agents and managers in our industry."
Nancy Mancuso, VP of Operations – International Modeling and Talent Association

"Clair Sinnett has enabled our graduates to achieve goals never before attainable. Through years of acting, teaching and coaching experience, Clair has developed the perfect acting curriculum. Thanks for helping us make our acting schools successful."
Domenic Camposeo, owner, Acting Conservatory Training Center (ACT), Toronto, Ontario, Canada, ICE Conservatory of Acting, Charlotte, North Carolina, U.S.

"Clair has a keen understanding of film and television and imparts the tools and knowledge students will need to compete in the worlds largest entertainment marketplace—Los Angeles."
Tracy Christian, agent – Peter Strain & Associates, Inc.

"The talent business is ever changing, but the one thing that remains unchanged is the quest for new talent. Even the most talented actors have to know how to get the audition. Understanding the marketing system in the entertainment business requires knowing how to 'get in' and how to be unique in today's crowded marketplace. Clair Sinnett's book shows you some of the paths for the serious actor to follow."
Helen Rogers, president emeritus – International Modeling and Talent Association

"Moving to Los Angeles and trying to figure out the business was insane! If it weren't for Clair and her marketing tools, I would have been lost!"
Gary Purdy, former student

Dedication

To my son, Brad, for always being supportive
To my parents, for believing I can do anything
To my 'girls,' who spent their time at my feet while I wrote this book
and
To the actors who share my passion.

Acknowledgements

Jackie Hart-Blanton, for getting me started
Douglas Gillis, for pushing me forward
Bradford Hill, my son, for getting the job done
and
My industry friends, who so graciously gave their words of wisdom!

Martin Barter
Judy Belshe
Breanna Benjamin
Melisa Birnstein
Nancy Moon-Broadstreet
Jan Brown
Richard DeLancy
Steve Eastin
Bruce Economou
Howard Fine
Barry Freed
Brian Funnagan
Laya Gelff
Irene Gilbert
Carolyn Thompson-Goldstein

Sonja Haney
Diane Hardin
Vaughn D. Hart
Vivian Hollander
Michael Jay
Ginger Lawrence
Stephen Laviska
Charity Marquis
Patty Grana-Miller
Bobby Moresco
Charles Nemes
Al Onorato
Linda Phillips-Palo
Brian Reise
Judy Savage

Jack Scagnetti
Josh Schiowitz
Myrl A. Schreibman
Brien Scott
TJ Stein
Jean St. James
Rodger Smith, Ph.D.
Stanzi Stokes
James F. Tarzia
Bill Treusch
Martin Weiss
Rosemary Welden
Dick Wieand
Halstan Williams

A Special Thanks To:

Neil Bagg
Jackie Hart-Blanton
Candi Barthelemy
Domenic Camposeo
Tommy Carrey
Tracy Christian
Mark Clausen
George Ferris

Kathleen Gibson
Alix Hart
Daniel Hepner
Will Jude
Swan Kim
Eddie Lamar
Keith Lewis
Beth Malone

Anthony Marini
Nancy Mancuso
Charles Matthau
Alan Mingo, Jr.
Richard Padro
PepsiCo
Melissa Petro
Garry Purdy

Aaron Revoir
Helen Rogers
Steve Schemmel
Robin Sydney
Michael Virut
Jed Weber
Lisa Wysocky

Table of Contents

Foreword

As you grow, there is nothing you can read and there's really nothing anyone can say that will make things like love, loss, and tragedy, any easier. However, as far as one's professional career is concerned, the sayings, "You have to learn for yourself" and "You learn from your mistakes" are sayings with which, for the most part, I disagree. It is not necessary to re-invent the wheel every time you set goals for yourself. That is the beauty of education, the wisdom of mentors, and the valuable insight of those in the know.

Clair is one of those "in the know." Her valuable insight and unique style of teaching has helped hundreds of professional actors "Take control of their own careers." *Clair's approach to **marketing** and the **business of acting** will surely help you take control of your career.*

I spent several years 'paying my dues' in this industry. I now work as a commercial producer/director. I have been fortunate to experience Clair's wisdom and unique perspective in academic, professional, and personal settings. I have been both an employer and employee of Clair's. She has motivated me to be successful and inspired me to be a better person. Clair is my mother, my mentor, and my friend. I'm certain that she will inspire you as well.

Best of luck,
Bradford Hill, producer/director/son
Commercial Works, L.A.

Introduction

Upon completion of my training as an actor, I realized that although I was well trained, I was not prepared to seek representation or auditions. What was lacking in my training was *marketing* and a clear understanding of the *business*. I wasted a lot of time learning 'the ropes.'

While performing in New York, I became more familiar with the business. I learned that other actors were experiencing the same lack of preparation I faced. Major theater conservatories and universities have never recognized the need to prepare actors with the necessary skills needed to obtain professional work as a performer. Actors are only prepared to perform. This was particularly evident when I crossed over to commercial casting and production, and even more evident when I became a SAG (Screen Actors Guild) franchised agent. The majority of my clients didn't have a clue how to market themselves. Providing they were even able to obtain representation, they expected their agent and/or manager to do it all, while they waited at home for the phone to ring.

As a casting director, it became even more evident to me that too many actors had become 'career acting students,' working at 'survival' jobs. Ultimately, they had accomplished nothing and had just ended up surviving. Unfortunately, many of these actors were talented. They just didn't know how to be seen or cast. They lacked the business and marketing skills needed to succeed.

This is what prompted me to develop a TV/film marketing and audition program. I started teaching workshops under my own banner, REAL to REEL, The Actors Workshop. Initially I marketed the actors in my workshops, while their agents collected the commission. It wasn't long before I became a SAG franchised agent, Clair Sinnett & Associates, Talent & Model Management. As I became more and more involved in casting and the casting community, I relocated to Los Angeles and opened Clair Sinnett Casting, while continuing to teach and direct. Today, I teach my TV/film marketing and TV/film acting programs throughout the U.S., Canada and Europe, as well as here in Los Angeles.

My students are prepared with their passion and training in one hand and their marketing and business skills in the other. My TV/film acting program has been taught at such prestigious schools and conservatories as the American Academy of Dramatic Arts, South Coast Repertory Conservatory, Playwrights Horizon Theater School, the National Academy of Television Arts and Sciences Repertory Group, University of California-Irvine, and is currently taught at the Acting Conservatory Training Center (ACT) in Toronto, Ontario and at the ICE Conservatory of Acting in Charlotte, North Carolina.

I have always felt that it should be mandatory for actors to take classes in marketing, business and advertising. Unfortunately, actors load themselves up with the art of the craft. They graduate with degrees and certificates from various performing arts centers and universities, yet are not at all prepared to enter the world of *show business*. Should they be offered a job, they are prepared to perform. However, they are not at all prepared to seek the job offers, nor to 'get in the door.'

The demand for a book to accompany my marketing and auditioning program and the ever-increasing demand for a TV/film marketing book for actors is what prompted me to write this book. I want to share my expertise, which is a product of a forty-year career in the business of entertainment.

We start with the premise that you are starting a business. The product that your business will develop and manufacture is 'YOU,' the actor. As with any business, the marketing, promotion, and sale of your product is crucial for your success. You will need to create exposure and generate interest in the market place; locate and find buyers and distributors; and motivate the consumers of your product to buy and re-buy your product, again and again. All of this begins with a *competent and professional marketing plan*.

Let's talk about *'getting in the door.'*

-Clair Sinnett

Act I

YOU AND YOUR BUSINESS

"If you don't get cast, no one ever gets
to see how talented you are."
-Clair

SCENE ONE
THE BUSINESS OF ACTING

The "GOLDEN AGE"

Hollywood has seen many changes in the past century. The one thing that has remained the same is its dominance in the motion picture and television business. Hollywood is the heart and soul of the entertainment industry. At the start of World War I, more than half of the motion pictures made were produced in Hollywood. During the war, film production throughout the world had come to a screeching halt, except in Hollywood. The 'Studio System' was born, and the absence of competition sparked the growth of Hollywood, as we know it.

By 1947, the American economy was at an all time high, and Hollywood was KING. The studio system, which consisted of the five majors: MGM, Paramount, Fox, Universal, and Warner Brothers, was more powerful than ever. In 1948, things changed. Studios began to feel the sting of the increasing popularity of television and box office revenues were down. The most notable change occurred with the Supreme Court's ruling in favor of the Justice Department. It was the Courts' opinion that the studios' ownership of theater chains violated Federal anti-trust laws. Subsequently, studios were forced to sell off their interests in theaters. This resulted ultimately in the end of the "Golden Age" of Hollywood. You could say that this was the event that paved the way for the emergence of independent studios and production companies, as we know them today. Studios no longer monopolized the exhibition and distribution of films.

Until this time, the studios placed actors under contract, frequently extending seven years or longer. Actors weren't cast for specific roles or films. They were contracted by individual studios to appear in several films. Needless to say, aspiring actors without a contract found it difficult to break into the film business.

The studios began to fragment and liquidate their holdings, ticket sales dropped, and Hollywood changed forever. One by one, actors started to challenge their contracts with the studios and were winning.

The business of acting had changed. A 'star's' talent and looks were no longer enough. The 'stars' now had competition. Agents were forced to put down their fat cigars, pull their feet off their desks, and earn their money. Actors would need to acquire certain business and marketing skills to be competitive.

Fifty years later, *business and marketing* skills have never been more important to the professional actor.

" . . . marketing can make or break someone's career. A fine example is Meryl Streep, who, when graduated from her Ivy League school, hired a publicist, not an agent or a manager."
Melisa Birnstein, manager
Associated Artists Management, L.A.
www.associatedartistsmngt.com

POSITIVE CHANGE

Today, along with the studios, networks, and production companies for whom they work, 'stars' employ armies of attorneys, agents, managers, PR people; and publicists to manage, publicize, market, and promote their careers and the films and TV shows they appear in. I am certain that Anthony Hopkins doesn't need my advice on marketing.

This book is about marketing and the business of acting. It is intended for both professional working actors that are looking to move to the next level, as well as those with aspirations of making acting a career. This is a book for any actor who wants to make a positive change in his life and career. **Positive change is created by opportunity. Opportunities are created by YOU.**

HOBBY OR PROFESSION

Acting can be a profession or a hobby. Only you can make that decision. Acting can be a wonderful hobby. Millions of people play baseball, softball, basketball, and a myriad of other sports as hobbies. They play for the love of the game. As far as hobbies go, acting is just as rewarding. However, those of you who choose to make acting a profession must be professional, stay professional, and treat acting as a business.

Actors should " . . . get the stars out of their eyes and get very focused and grounded. This is a business and like any business you need a plan, focus, determination, and flexibility. Some of the best actors (will never be seen) because they don't have the business gene. . . . actors that are household names are where they are because of their perseverance and tenacity."
Rosemary Welden, CSA, casting director
L.A.

More Than a Full-Time Job . . .

"Showbiz" is extremely competitive. Acting is a business. Being a professional actor means being in business for yourself. You are starting your own business. Starting and managing your business will require the same amount of time and commitment that any other business would require to be successful.

> *"I expect my clients to treat this business as a full time, forty-hour a week job. It's the only way to succeed in this business. Whether they're studying in class, working out, doing a show . . . it all adds up to making them a better actor."*
> **Bruce Economou, manager**
> **John Crosby Management, L.A.**

> *"What attracts you to the profession? Make sure you're not seduced by the amounts of money certain actors are paid. Ultimately, one should want to be an artist. If money is the main reason, go play Major League Baseball."*
> **Al Onorato, manager**
> **Handprint Entertainment, L.A.**

When you make the decision to become a professional actor, you must be willing to devote at least forty hours a week to your career. And unless you are a lottery winner, you will likely have another full-time job as well.

On top of your living expenses, you will have expenses for your acting career. Becoming a professional actor is expensive. You will need to budget and set aside money every month for classes, workshops, showcases, pictures, mailings, etc. If you are planning on relocating to Los Angeles or New York, I recommend having enough money saved up to cover at least six months of living and business expenses.

> *"If you can do something else and be happy, do it. It's much too hard to do what we do."*
> **Bobby Moresco, writer/director**
> **The Actors Gym, L.A.**

YOUR BUSINESS

Let's set up an entertainment company: your 'Business.' You may have already sold stock in your company. By that I mean, your family and friends may have purchased shares of stock in your business by giving or lending you money to assist with living expenses, training, pictures, etc. I'm sure that my parents, at various times early in my career, owned more shares of stock in my business than I did. If you haven't already sold stock in your business, now is a good time to do so.

We will leave 'luck' out of the equation for now, and focus on the basics needed for your success. If you are going to make it in this business of show, you need to have an advantage over the thousands of other professional actors competing for YOUR job.

YOUR PRODUCT

You are going into business for yourself. You're going into *show business*, and the product is 'YOU.' Like every business, *marketing* your product is crucial. The public has to know what your product is, why it's different, and where to find it. Most of all, they must want it.

> *"Marketing is important to the professional actor, whether beginner or star. The difference is the methods used for marketing. The star obviously has it easier and has the means with which to market themselves properly. The beginner has to market him/herself to those who can lead them to jobs. Getting the right picture is key, as this is your calling card. Then getting your face (your calling card) in front of people is often up to you, the actor."*
> **Josh Schiowitz, agent**
> **Schiowitz, Clay, Ankrum & Ross, Inc., L.A.**

The product that your business will *manufacture*, *market*, and *sell* is you, the actor. Now that you know what your product is, you must define it.

ACT II

THE PRODUCT 'YOU'

"The most difficult role you'll ever play is yourself."
-Clair

SCENE TWO
DEFINE YOUR PRODUCT

STEREOTYPES AND CASTING

You must define your product so that everyone will know exactly what *'type'* of product you are selling. By everyone, I am referring to potential distributors, buyers, and consumers of your product.

The market tends to stereotype, so keep this in mind. A nine-year-old kid should look like what we expect a nine-year-old to look like (freckles, cap, jeans and a T-shirt). A grandmother should look like what we expect a grandmother to look like (grey hair in a bun with glasses), not what many grandmothers really look like today. Fortunately, there are some advertisers that are now realizing that seniors are hipper and younger looking today than they were in the sixties. However, for the most part, we want to see Betty White baking cookies, not Diane Cannon.

> " . . . stereotyping sounds so bad. It's typecasting, and it's how this
> business works. Clients don't like guess work. They want viewers
> to recognize and identify with characters immediately. It's much
> easier for people in New York or Los Angeles to accept a Mom
> baking a pie and wearing an apron, than it is for Middle America
> to accept a mom with a mohawk, riding a motorcycle."
> **Bradford Hill, producer/director**
> **Commercial Works, L.A.**

Casting, for the most part, has always been—and will probably always be—stereotypical. It's not Hollywood's fault. The viewing audience, in general, has a lazy imagination; it's too much for them to accept the role of an accountant to be played by anyone but an overweight guy with glasses. When the viewing audience looks at the film screen or glances at the TV, they expect and accept stereotyped characters. If I were to cast Arnold Schwarzenegger in the role of a mailman, the public would never buy it—it would take too much thought. Besides, we want Arnold to be our hero and save us from the bad guys, not deliver the mail. The audience needs to recognize the floor polishing mom, the tired construction worker, and the supermodel eating low-fat corn chips.

"Unfortunately, there are more opportunities for actors that easily fit stereotypical roles. Breakdowns are very specific, 'blonde, athletic, American.' But, I will fight for clients that aren't stereotypical."
Bill Treusch, manager
Bill Treusch Associates, N.Y.

'TYPE' CASTING

Stereotypical casting, or *'typecasting,'* is often different in films than in television or commercials. In films, the director often has ninety minutes or more to develop the characters. Although *'counter casting'* (going against type) is sometimes used in films, the majority of roles are type cast.

In The Lead . . .

In television, the 'lead' characters should be recognized in the first five minutes of screen time. Of course, there are always exceptions to the rule. Sometimes there's a plot twist, or a character's evil intentions are revealed at the end of the show. You will see this a lot in soap operas because it's a way to get the viewers to tune in the next day. However, the audience needs to identify the 'good guys' from the 'bad guys;' in other words, who's wearing the white hat and who's wearing the black hat.

Needed Support . . .

In film, the characters with whom the leads come in contact are called *'supporting roles.'* In television, they are referred to as *'guest stars'* or *'featured roles.'* These characters need to be immediately recognizable, and are usually the most stereotypical roles in TV.

Supporting roles are often the roles that the series regulars interact with in the course of the story. The director doesn't have time to develop the role of the cab driver or the waitress. The audience needs to know who they are right away. In daytime television, these roles usually have few lines, and are referred to as *'day players.'* On the East Coast, they are referred to as *'U 5's'* (under 5 lines). Day Player and Under 5, refer to the types of union contracts actors sign when cast.

An actor whose type is easily identified will usually have an easier time working in television. By developing your *type*, you will create a need for your product. There are actors who make a living playing the roles of cops or lawyers. That is their type, because their look and demeanor is believable. There are young female actors that are typically cast as the *'vixen,'* the sexy teen with the great hair and body. Likewise, there are other young female actors that typically play the *'ingénue,'* the girl your mom wants you to date. Either type is necessary to tell a story.

The Other Woman . . .

When I was a young actress starting out, I was always cast as the *'other woman.'* I was never the ingénue. My look was too sophisticated and my voice was always 'throaty.' I just wasn't believable as the *'young innocent.'* The bright side for me, personally, was that the roles in which I was cast were always more fun.

Typecasting is not necessarily a bad thing, so don't fight it. If you think about it, almost every story has the stereotypical gang-member, judge, jock, or doctor to name a few. Once you define your type, your *product*, you will soon find yourself working a lot more than those whose type is not easily defined or recognizable.

> *"There are more opportunities for actors that easily fit stereotypical roles."*
> **Stephen Laviska, agent**
> **Lally Talent Agency, N.Y.**

Mom . . . I'm Home!

In commercials, viewers have about five seconds to recognize your type and know who you are. Are you the jock, nerd, girl next door, mom, or dad? Advertisers have thirty to sixty seconds to sell their product. They want to spend that time selling soft drinks, not developing the character of an over-worked and under-paid ad executive, whose answer to a hard day is a refreshing beverage. If you fit the stereotype of an ad executive, spend less time trying to be a pirate.

YOUR 'TYPE'

When you are just starting out, it is very important to explore and discover what type you actually are. Get to be known as one of the best actors of your type. It's all about looks, so ask yourself what sort of character you portray best and what sort of message the camera will get from your special looks?

If your *type* is a school kid, be a school kid. Look like a kid: no makeup, no frills, no shirt and tie. Dress the way you go out the door for school or to play. If you're seventeen years old or younger, you are a minor and should look like a minor. There will be plenty of opportunities to play 'sexy' when you're an adult. Enjoy looking your age. Be natural. Avoid sophisticated hairstyles and clothing.

If you happen to be a computer nerd or a jock, go with it. If you have extreme tastes in clothing and hairstyles, use that too. Be comfortable, don't costume; just do 'your thing.'

This is called your *'camera character.'* It's typecasting. Take advantage of it. After you've been cast regularly as your type and have made a name for yourself, then you can begin to branch out and go against your type.

Tom Hanks went against his comedic type and won an Academy Award for his role in *Philadelphia*. Meg Ryan went against her romantic comedy type when she starred in *When a Man Loves a Woman*. Both actors had established careers before they went against their types. Had they challenged their type earlier in their careers, they may have met with less success.

Actors are more often typed for television than for film. A major film star like Tom Cruise usually does one or two films a year. He delivers a total of two to five hours of screen time a year. Kelsey Grammer, on the other hand, is *Frasier* every week. Tom Cruise can make adjustments and show different facets of his personality in various roles, such as *Born on the Fourth of July* and *Vanilla Sky*. Kelsey Grammer is expected to be Frasier week after week. His character is what the TV audience loves, appreciates, and continues to invite into their homes year after year.

The following exercise will assist you with the development of your product by helping you define your type.

EXERCISE #1

Use the worksheet in the back of the book to help you determine your *'type.'* It's important to be specific, keeping stereotypical casting in mind. Your type (your product) must be immediately recognizable. Your age or the age you look will be an important factor in defining your product. Your style of dress, hairstyle, make-up, personality, the way you walk, sit, and laugh are all special qualities and quirks that create your image—*the product*.

What *type* are you? What types of roles do you see yourself being cast in, and why? Ask four friends, four family members, and four people that you don't know well the same questions. Is there a pattern?

*Use your judgment when talking to people with whom you are unfamiliar. I recommend friends of friends, friends of family members, or other students.

**Minors/children should NOT speak to strangers, or anyone outside their family or circle of friends without parental supervision.

SCENE THREE
REFINE YOUR PRODUCT

TRAINING

Now that you have defined your product, you must *refine* your product. Refining your product means making yourself the best you can be. Education, acting workshops, fitness training, voice, dance, and diction classes are crucial to your success. If you haven't already, take the time to be trained in your craft.

> "*First and foremost, learn the craft of the actor.* Become good at
> what you do. Then and only then, learn the business of acting.
> . . . you now have something to offer, something to be proud of,
> (and) something to be confident of. A word of absolute
> caution to the young artist, invert the above and you'll be lost forever."
> **Bobby Moresco, writer/director**
> **The Actors Gym, L.A.**

Training is not something that you stop. Rock stars rehearse and professional athletes work out to stay in shape. The professional actor must continue to fine-tune his craft by trying new things. True champions, stars, and professionals are never satisfied; they continually strive to improve. An excellent example would be Jay Leno. One of the most successful and recognizable faces on TV, Mr. Leno regularly performs at a comedy club not far from my home in Southern California. My guess is that he doesn't need the pay or exposure. He likely performs to keep his stand-up skills sharp and to try out new material. He strives for excellence.

> "Every professional athlete, singer, dancer, artist continues to
> train throughout their career. I've never heard of an actor that
> got turned down for a job because they had too much training."
> **Brian Reise, acting coach**
> **Brian Reise Acting Studios, L.A.**

Grow Up!

Actors need to continually hone their skills, to stretch and grow in their craft. The way to do this is by attending classes and workshops. Workshops and classes are especially important when you're not working on a project. That's when you attend a workshop or class, because that's when you need them the most. When you are cast, drop out of your workshop and focus on your work. Rejoin your workshop when your job is wrapped. This way, you are continually working—if not on a project, then in class or a workshop.

> *"An actor always needs to exercise . . . to stretch themselves . . .*
> *to approach their craft from many perspectives, and to always*
> *remember that 'acting is so simple, it is difficult.' The actor's*
> *instinct and the honest impulses that they use to motivate dialogue*
> *needs exercising to be on their game."*
> **Myrl A. Schreibman, acting coach/teacher**
> **The Strasberg Institute, L.A.**

Gotta Start Somewhere . . .

There are a myriad of classes and workshops for the professional actor. For example, there are workshops and classes in scene study, cold reading and audition techniques, improvisation, commercial and TV/film acting, voice and diction, stand-up comedy, musical theater, combat and stunt, soap and sitcom acting, voice over, and technique training that are readily available.

> *"I always encourage an actor to start with their 'reason' for taking*
> *a class. What is their goal and will this particular class help them to*
> *achieve it? If you are going to focus on commercials, take a commercial*
> *class. If you are going to do plays, then take a theatre class. If you want*
> *to work in film and television, take a class that will teach you about the*
> *'business' and provide you with a venue for practicing audition technique.*
> *Be specific and make sure the class teaches what it offers."*
> **Brian Reise, acting coach**
> **Brian Reise Acting Studios, L.A.**

If you have not already trained in a specific technique, you may want to start with a technique class.

ACTING TECHNIQUES

What is an *acting technique*? It's a method of procedure. It's a way to go from point A to point B. For example, technique training would be extremely helpful if you were cast in the role of a young mother with a sick child, and have never had any children of your own. Using an acting technique, with the added support of your creative imagination, would hopefully enable you to portray the role believably.

> *"A technique is made up of the tools that help an actor create characters that are not only memorable, but appropriate to the playwright's intentions and ideas. An actor must work on a technique so that he/she can continuously develop such characters throughout years of work and thus build a body of memorable, informed characters. To that end, technique is work, but that frees up the actor. Technique must become invisible; the audience must not be aware of the actor's technique. Some approach a role through reading the play, understanding the ideas of the play, and then applying one's imagination to creating an appropriate character. This is what the 'Stella Adler Technique' is based upon. An actor must research the technique they are auditing and decide if it is an approach that will work for them. They should find out which actors have studied and continue to use that technique. Remember as Miss Adler said, 'Classes should help the actor become responsible for his/her own artistic achievement and development, so choose your classes wisely. Your artistic achievement and development are on the line'."*
> **Irene Gilbert, academy director**
> **The Stella Adler Academy, L.A.**

I Recall . . .

'Emotional Recall' or *'Affective Memory'* is an inner technique taught by Strasberg. It is a technique that still works for me today. Years ago in New York, I was cast as a young mother with a dying child. I had never experienced motherhood or the overwhelming love you have for your own child. So, I used *Emotional Recall*. I 'recalled' my childhood experience of losing my dog. At that time in my life experience, that was my greatest loss. The

downside of this technique is that the older I get, the more painful experiences I have to recall. The bright side is there are far more experiences that are positive.

Don't Get Lost . . .

Think of a technique like a map. If you want to travel from Los Angeles to San Francisco, there are a variety of routes to drive. For example, you could drive up the coast on Pacific Coast Highway or you could take the 'scenic' 5 Freeway through barren desert, where you'll find a few scattered orange groves and pig farms. There are also other modes of transportation available. You could take a plane, train, bus, bicycle, motorcycle, etc.

No matter which route or mode of transportation you take, the end result will be that you have traveled from Los Angeles to San Francisco. You may arrive at different times or on different days, but you'll get there. Much like the choice of technique, no matter what technique you choose or how long it takes, you will learn to portray that young mom with a sick child believably and make the role yours.

There are many good technique classes. Some coaches offer classes based upon their own techniques, while others are disciples of the *'Masters.'* You'll find a list of recommended technique classes in the back of the book.

THE MASTERS

Many good teachers offer classes based on a specific technique of one of the Masters, while many borrow a little from each.

The following is a brief introduction to the better-known 'Masters' and their techniques.

Constantin Stanislavski: The 'Father' of acting techniques as we know them today. Strasberg, Meisner, and Adler, were part of the original *Group Theater*, and all studied Stanislavski. Each came away with his own interpretation of Stanislavski's work and created his own method or technique. Thankfully, disciples of these great Master Teachers continue to teach their work today. There are also a few noted newcomers. For more information: **www.alltheaterarts.com/article1043.html.**

Lee Strasberg (Actors Studio): Strasberg is best known for his inner work, referred to as *The Method*. The Method is a technique based upon expressing deep emotion and then controlling that emotion by opening up the actor's emotional life. For more information: **www.theactorsstudio.com** or The Strasberg Institute: **www.strasberg.com/hollywood.**

Sanford Meisner (Neighborhood Playhouse): Meisner used the bond between scene partners. His technique focused on communication and the actor's imagination. Scene partners played off one another's responses using his 'Word Repetition' to change emotions. For more information: **www.the-neiplay.org** or **www.themeisnercenter.com.**

Stella Adler (Stella Adler Conservatory): Adler used the author's text. Uniting the actor's imagination and his role within the boundaries of the text, her technique combined the words with the given circumstances. For more information: **www.stellaadler.com.**

Viola Spolin (Young Actors Company): Spolin was the originator of *improvisation*. Solving a problem without a script or storyline forces you to be in each moment with your scene partner, because the future is unknown. For more information: **www.spolin.com/violabio** or The Spolin Center: **www.spolin.com/ny-vs-chic.html.**

Uta Hagan (HB Studios): Hagan recreates reality through exploration of circumstances to bring truth to the scene. She uses 'moment to moment' exercise work. The Howard Fine Studio in Los Angeles brings this great lady in from New York as a yearly guest. For more information: **www.wic.org/bio/hagan.html.**

Other Masters worth mentioning are:
Tadashi Susuki (The Theater of Grandeur): www.siti.org/workshops.html
Michael Chekhov (Chekhov Theater Ensemble): www.pharo.com/chekhov.html
F. Matthias Alexander (The Alexander Technique): www.alexandertechnique.com
Maria Ouspenskaya (American Lab):
www.blockbuster.com/bb/person/details/0,7621,bio-p+54458,00.html

Whichever path you eventually choose to take with your training, I always recommend familiarizing yourself with the various techniques of the Masters.

So Many Techniques, So Little Time

Because there are so many techniques from which to choose, it is important to audit a variety of classes. Familiarize yourself with different teachers and their training methods. Once you digest the various techniques, put them to the test. Select a monologue, and then apply the exercises that you learned from the various technique classes. Which technique made the work easier and more enjoyable? Eventually, you will find a technique that works best for you.

A technique will help actors " . . . bring their personal experience and depth to the work truthfully. I've studied many techniques with many teachers: Uta Hagen, Bobby Lewis, Stella Adler, The Actors Studio, Herbert Bergdorf Studio and others. They were all good. The difference with Sandy's technique was it made me more real, truthful. The others made me think instead of feel. Sandy's technique made me real. I used my own depth to get a more truthful performance."
Martin Barter, artistic director of The Sanford Meisner Center, L.A.
Head Teacher of The Meisner/Carville School of Acting, L.A.
www.themeisnercenter.com

You may choose one technique, or you may borrow a little from each. For example, I'm *'method'* based, but I find that I use a variety of techniques to get to where I need to be. The best technique of all is *"whatever works."*

"I agree, but young actors take this ("whatever works") to mean 'whatever is easiest.' To use a technique, you must first master it. It's like a little knowledge. It gets you into more trouble.
Roger Smith, Ph.D., acting option coordinator
Assoc. Professor, Dep't. of Theater and Dance
Ball State University

When deciding on an acting technique, "See what (technique) speaks to and works for you. Goethe once said, 'We only acquire that which we put into practice.'"
Howard Fine, acting coach
Howard Fine Acting Studio, L.A.

WORKSHOPS AND CLASSES

Once you have learned a technique, or while you are learning, you will need to apply what you have learned within a scene study class. Often, the school, studio, or teacher with whom you study technique will also offer a subsequent scene study class. If you decide to take scene study classes at a different studio, ask for the teachers training resume. It is important for you to know where they studied, with whom they studied, and which techniques they use. After you have audited several scene study workshops and classes, you will have a better idea of where you belong and which technique you prefer.

> *"When considering acting classes, a person should do his/her homework—learn which coaches have working clients, how long has the acting coach been teaching, how many legitimate agents and managers send their clients to that coach."*
> **Martin Weiss, manager**
> **ETS Management, L.A.**

> When auditing classes, *" . . . take note of the teacher/coach and the quality of the results that he/she gets from the actors in the workshop. Many people who run classes are actors attempting to make a living, and are not able to communicate to other actors what an actor needs."* Take a look at *" . . . the other actors in the workshop: who are they? Are they excellent in what they do? Are they people you want to work with?"*
> **Myrl A. Schreibman, acting coach/teacher**
> **Strasberg Institute, L.A.**

> *"Avoid any training that attempts to have you be psychoanalyzed by someone who is imminently unqualified."*
> **Steve Eastin, acting coach**
> **Steve Eastin Studio, L.A.**

You may prefer a class to a workshop. A class is usually a six- to twelve-week course. It has a beginning, middle, and end. When the class is finished, you can enroll in your next class of choice. A workshop is on-going and open-ended. You usually pay on a month-to-month basis. Actors attend as frequently or infrequently as their work schedules permit. Whether you choose a class or a workshop, look for a teacher that directs the actors to be natural and believable. Conversational dialogue is a must.

"The atmosphere should be nurturing and creative, yet disciplined. Check to see if the students and teacher have respect for their work. How do the students interact with the teacher? Is there trust? Does the teacher have insight into the student's problems? Are the critiques clear and to the point?"
Howard Fine, acting coach
Howard Fine Acting Studio, L.A.

I think two years of scene study with any good teacher is sufficient. Then move on to another style and technique. This way you will eventually develop your own unique style and technique. There are some actors who become 'career students' of one specific teacher. They are acting students, but they are not necessarily actors. Don't fall into the guru following.

I am a strong believer in acting/scene study workshops. A scene study workshop is the study of scenes or monologues with a scene partner. Some teachers/directors prefer that you rehearse with your scene partner outside of the workshop. Their opinion is that actors learn from the rehearsal process. Others believe that each actor should prepare on his own and come in ready to perform the scene fresh. Their reasoning is that when you are cast, you will most likely arrive on set without the benefit of rehearsal with your partner, so you should get used to preparing on your own. Both approaches work.

The Spa…

A workshop is like a spa. Actors go to workshops to keep their acting muscles strong and workout their skills. You've got to work out, keep yourself fit. An actor is at his best when he's working. An actor auditions best when he's working or performing. There's no time to get stale; he stays fresh and alive. The time to train is when you are not working on a project or performing, so that you can keep your skills sharp and ready. You know what happens to that great body when you stop working out. That's what happens to the actor's edge, the sharpness *turns to flab*!

"Good training both frees and challenges the actor. It is like working out. It keeps you in shape."
Howard Fine, acting coach
Howard Fine Acting Studio, L.A.

I suggest that you audit several workshops/classes to compare personality, teaching style, and technique. **<u>Don't be afraid to ask questions.</u>**

- **What does the instructor expect from students inside and outside of the classroom?** You'll need to know how much time you will need to commit.

- **Do you work every session?** You learn by observing, but starting out you may learn more by doing.

- **Are your scenes and scene partners assigned or do you find your own?** Do you work better in a structured environment with assigned material and partners? Finding the right material for you and matching up with a partner that also likes the material can be frustrating.

- **Do you rehearse inside or outside of the classroom environment?** Your time may or may not be limited. Rehearsing on your own enables you to discover and grow with your scene partner. Working with the scene unrehearsed and performing fresh with your scene partner recreates the demands of a working environment. Eventually you will know which environment is best for you. I learned the craft rehearsing outside of the classroom and now I prefer an unstructured environment such as The Actors Gym.

- **Do you perform the same scene each week until you and the director are satisfied?** You may learn more perfecting the scene.

- **What level are the actors in the class?** You will certainly learn more working with experienced actors, but will they want to spend time working with a beginner? Usually a teacher will audition an actor and place him/her in the appropriate class level. In a technique class, everyone is learning a new technique, so levels may not be so important.

You will find a list of recommended scene study workshops and classes, for both the east and west coasts in the back of the book.

UNIVERSITY TRAINING

You may want to consider formal training. Universities offer degreed programs, good training and the opportunity to learn while performing on stage. Of course that degree offers you additional employment options, and as my son once told me, "University prepares you for life. It prepares you for simply walking into a room and handling yourself in any situation."

"There are several reasons (for actors to consider university training), but the major one is basic training. If it is a good university system and it is one that understands what the camera and/or the stage professions demand, that is the business of acting, then that four years gives you the opportunity to lay down the basics of acting and to grow. Life is required of most actors; that is a life lived. If they jump too early, with no knowledge and no support system, no money and no understanding of life on their own, then their chances are not even close to good. Going to university will not guarantee the actor will make it, but without a solid understanding of the basics of acting and the basics of the business, then I can pretty much guarantee the actor won't 'make it.' Are there exceptions? Sure, but your chances of being the exception are better with the state lottery than acting in film and TV without some sort of road map.

Actors are independent businesses and that business needs to be lean and mean. They must develop their product (classes, work in acting), but importantly they must market that product. What most young actors do not understand is the business. They are not prepared for the profession and how long it takes to develop a network, market the product, and wisely use of capital earned and borrowed. In fact most become actors so they won't have to think about such things, but it is such thinking that improves their odds and extends their life in the business. A good university system, like the one at Ball State University, helps them develop their first tool kit for the art and business of acting. If it doesn't, then don't go there.

Once finished with university, they are prepared to move to L.A. or N.Y. and to design the next stage in their education. I call that 'Practical Theatre 101.' But they shouldn't be fooled into thinking that the learning is over. It never ends. They still need to work to enhance the execution of their craft and to develop the business of applying that craft to the professional world."
Roger Smith, Ph.D., acting option coordinator
Assoc. Professor, Dep't. of Theater and Dance
Ball State University

When choosing a university, visit and audit classes. See performances and get a list of celebrity alumni. Does their work excite you? Were you duly impressed by the student performances? Were the classes you visited exciting and informative? Did the campus feel comfortable? Do you want to be there for four years for a BA or BFA? Do you want to devote an additional three years for an MFA? Were the professors approachable? Were you able to visit the dorms and talk with the students? Do they offer industry showcases on both coasts? If they do, are they well attended? Do you want to spend the next four or five years studying at a university, or do you want to take advantage of your youth and attend a two-year conservatory in New York or Los Angeles? Just remember that a degree will always give you something to fall back on and is still well respected.

A good book to have is the *Directory of Theater Training Programs* edited by Jill Charles. You will enjoy learning more about the varied programs available to you that come with a degree and/or certification.

There are many college and university programs to consider. Look up *University Theater and TV/film Training Programs* and the *Consortium of Conservatory Theater Training Programs* at http://www.ncarts.edu/drama/. I have also put together a recommended list of universities that offer theater and TV/film B.F.A. and M.F.A. programs, in the back of this book.

CONSERVATORIES

Many professional performing arts schools offer two-year programs specializing in the performing arts in a conservatory environment. A conservatory environment is a place for preserving the craft and growing in that discipline. During your four to eight hour days you will concentrate on the different areas of the performing arts. There are no subjects taught that are not directly related to the performing arts. Your days may consist of dance, voice, improvisation, scene study, technique, combat, movement, fencing, speech, musical theatre, classics, rehearsal, etc. The programs are very much the same as a B.F.A. or M.F.A. program; however, the concentration is on the performing arts of choice. There are no math, history, or geography classes.

I suggest that you visit the school and audit classes the same way as discussed with universities. Talk with students and find out whom the alumni are. Do they offer an industry showcase upon graduation? Do they offer a certificate of graduation? Are they accredited and/or affiliated with an accredited university? Should you choose to return to an accredited university to complete your degree, you will have a head start.

You will find a list of a few well-known conservatories on both coasts that offer certificates or AA degrees in the back of this book. You can research these programs on the internet and obtain more information from the *National Association of Schools of Theater* at **http://www.artsacredit.org/nast/default.htm.**

Shop Around . . .

Do your homework. Acting is a business of emotions; don't place your talent and your emotions with just anyone. Shop around. Audit classes. Visit the campus. Ask questions.

When you see an actor's work that you admire, ask them with whom and where they studied. Look up the bios of established actors to see with whom they studied. After you attend an equity waiver play in Los Angeles or an off off-Broadway production in New York City, go back stage. Ask the actors who impressed you, with whom they studied. It won't be long before you have a list of classes and techniques to audit. You can also look up teachers and university faculty on the internet.

Asking agents, casting directors and managers who they recommend is also an excellent way to find just the right technique and the right teacher for you.

"Before choosing a performing arts school, an actor must do a lot of homework. Find out the schools track record. Who are the teachers— read their résumés, have they worked as actors or have they only 'studied' acting? What classes are taught as part of the program? Who has studied there? Can an actor take individual classes or does an actor have to sign up for the full program? Is the program accredited by a board of higher or secondary education (State, Federal, etc.)? And above all, try to audit a class. Is the teacher professional? Pretentious? Do they allow for input from the student actors—which is a sign of encouraging the actor's own development. Are the actors willing to take risks? Are the students respectful of one another? What is your over-all feel of the class and of the place in general? You should see a disciplined, yet creative and open environment. You should see that the focus is on the student actors and the work, not on the teacher. And finally, you have to trust your instincts. If you feel good about the program, then try it. If not, move on to the next program on your list."
Irene Gilbert, academy director
Stella Adler Academy, L.A.

You'll find a list of teachers and coaches in the back of this book. I highly recommend that you take a look at *The Hollywood Acting Coaches and Teachers Directory* by Lawrence Parke and *Where to Train* by Keith Wolfe.

EXERCISE #2

Using the worksheet in the back of the book, make a list of programs from which you would be interested in obtaining information. Once you have obtained information about the various programs of interest via mail or the internet, go back to your list and mark the programs that you would be interested in auditing. Remember, reputable programs will let you audit for free.

SCENE FOUR
IMAGE AND PACKAGING

PRODUCT IMAGE AND PACKAGING

Once you have **defined** and **refined** your product, you must decide how to package that product to best show off your **type** before putting it on the market. Next time you're in a grocery store, walk down the cereal aisle and look at the packaging of the various brands of cereal. The intention is to tell you the contents by the looks of their container. As you walk through aisle after aisle of the grocery store looking for various items, there are certain packages that catch your eye, causing you to pick one brand over another. Whether it be color, shape, adornment, size, etc., it's all *image and packaging*.

The packager has created an image and packaged the product to create a demand from the consumer. With your business, you want to package your product—YOU—to show agents, managers, and casting directors what's inside and create the demand for your product. We all want to know what we're buying before we buy it. Just as you try on shoes before choosing the right pair to go with an outfit; agents, managers, and casting directors will interview and audition your product to be sure that it will go with the rest of the cast.

YOUR PRODUCT'S IMAGE AND PACKAGING

The way you package your product is important. It's your image. It's how the consumer perceives you. The way you dress, the way you accessorize, and the way you look are how you package yourself. This is how you show off your **type**, so that the consumer knows what he is buying.

Look in the mirror. Do you see the product that you want to sell? Is this what you really want to sell? Refer to worksheet #1 in Scene 2 where you defined your product. Does your packaging reflect your product, your type? Refer to the list of roles and types you have prepared. Does the mirror reflect the roles that you have defined for yourself?

A Hard Look...

Adults especially, really need to take a hard look at themselves. Does your image convey your type? How can you be sold? Are you a young professional or a mom? Are you blue collar or white collar, a doctor or a used car salesman? How do you fit in? Because camera work is visual, from the time you walk in the door, you need to look like who you are. Does your image reflect the roles that you defined in your earlier exercises?

Yes, we are all versatile and feel many different things. There are many facets to our personalities, and actors always believe that they can do it all. That's true, but lets establish your niche. If it's a sit-com leading man, then become the best sit-com leading man you can be before you start challenging your type as an actor. Start with your type. An agent can sell a type; a manager can develop you as that type; and the casting director will cast you as that type. Have a starting point.

ACT YOUR AGE!

If you're a minor, your packaging (your dress) should be that of a 'kid.' Look like a kid—no frills, just jeans and a T-shirt. Girls should wear little or no make-up. Lip-gloss and mascara is all that's needed. There is **no** benefit for a minor to look older than eighteen. In fact, it will work against you. Because of child labor laws and union rules, it is much more expensive to hire a minor than it is to hire an adult. A minor has to have a parent or guardian on set at all times, as well as a teacher provided by the production company. The production also needs to provide an additional trailer or room to be used as a classroom, all of which is paid by the production company. The greatest cost of all is the loss of work time, time in front of the camera. Depending upon age, the hours that a minor can work are limited. The producer must provide time for rest and schoolwork. Identical twins are appealing because producers can double the character's camera time. No one is going to cast a fifteen-year-old that looks eighteen. It would be wise for the stage mothers of the world to save the 'Brittany' costumes for October 31st.

Eighteen to Play Younger . . .

A producer will cast an eighteen-year-old that looks fifteen. There's a wonderful window called 'eighteen to play younger.' If you fit into this window, you have an advantage because minors cost more. A prominent producer once told me that "the savings in meals alone is reason enough" to cast eighteen to play younger. He says that "most minors come to work with two parents and a teacher" and "at sixty dollars a day per person, a minor who works thirty days on a project could cost an additional $7200 in meals alone."

Should the production go on location, the production company must provide first class, round trip airfare for the parents or guardian, and a studio teacher, as well as a hotel room for each. Even if the minor wants to share a room with a parent or guardian, the minor still must have his own room. So if the production company is paying for a minor, you had better look like one.

EXERCISE #3

Using the worksheet in the back of the book, make a list of all the commercials in which you could see yourself. Now make a list of all the TV programs in which you see yourself. Next, make a list of the film roles for which you think you would have been right.

Compare types, paying close attention to dress, roles, and styles of shows. Do you see a pattern? Are you getting closer to the type you will be auditioning for?

Recognizing your type and the style of show you are seeking is important. You must know exactly what type you are before you can market and sell your product. Know your product and your optimum market.

ACT III

THE MARKET

"It's Show BUSINESS, not Show ART."
-Clair

SCENE FIVE
THE INDUSTRY AND YOU

BUSINESS IS BUSINESS

As we have discussed, starting and managing your business requires the same commitment that any other small business would require. Business is business. The process of starting, managing, marketing, advertising, promoting, and selling your product, as well as the creative, administrative, managerial, marketing, advertising, promotional, and sales specialists with whom you will need to surround yourself to be successful, parallels that of any other business—big or small.

> I " . . . look for an actor who treats his/her career like a business; an actor who takes this business seriously and will be the hardest working member of their team. It's the only way they'll be successful."
> **Bruce Economou, manager**
> **John Crosby Management, L.A.**

THE 'BIZ' IN SHOWBIZ:

You will set up your business, sell stock, and invest in your company to create a product. Again, the product that your company will create is YOU. You are the product. You made the product. You are the *manufacturer*. You will define and refine your product. You will develop an image and package your product. The next step is preparing to put your product on the market.

The *'end users,'* or the people that will ultimately buy your product, are consumers. The consumers purchase theater and movie tickets, rent videos and DVDs, and watch TV programming and commercials. You have to get your product to the consumers. The consumers will ultimately dictate your product's *market demand*; however, the purpose of this book is to market your product in order to create an *industry demand*. Only you can create the demand for your product within the industry.

As an actor, you don't tap-dance door-to-door down Main St., USA in an effort to sell yourself as an actor. A company that manufactures widgets doesn't go door-to-door selling its products. Most likely, they don't call on every retail store that would carry their product, either. A manufacturer uses a *'middle-man.'* The middleman would be a wholesaler or distributor. Actors use agents and managers as *distributors*. Agents and managers distribute your product—YOU—to casting directors.

All retail stores employ **buyers**. Buyers follow trends, trying to determine which products are hot and which are not. Casting directors are the buyers. They work for production companies, studios and networks. The production companies, studios and networks are the **retail outlets** that sell your product to the consumers. You see? It's just a business.

Make Room on the Shelf!

Retail outlets have limited shelf space. If a certain product doesn't sell, it is discontinued and replaced with another product. Just because a product does not sell, doesn't mean it's not a good product. It may have been marketed poorly. If the public isn't tuning in to see a particular show, the show is cancelled and replaced. If the public isn't standing in line to see a particular actor's films or plays, there will be less demand for that actor in the future.

Biggest BANG for the Buck!

Production companies, studios and networks, like all businesses, want to put the best product for the least amount of money on the market. Having the best possible product is important in a competitive market to obtain the largest possible share of the consumer's dollars. Spending as little as possible to get your product from conception to the marketplace is important to every business. It's how profits are determined.

Actors are usually cast for one of three reasons. The first is the actor's 'star factor' or name recognition. The second is whether or not the actor is right for the role, i.e.: talent, looks, age, etc. And lastly is whom the actor knows or is related to. We will discuss the first two.

Actors are often cast based on their name value. The bigger the star, the more viewers or ticket buyers. Consumers won't pay to see *Mission Impossible 5* because of the cool story line; they will pay to see Tom Cruise. Tom Cruise is expensive. For his films to see profits, production companies and studios must sell far more tickets and DVDs than a film without Tom Cruise. The market demand of Tom Cruise dictates the supply and cost of his films.

Another reason that actors are cast is that they are right for the roles. Actors without bankable names, such as Chris Cooper, are usually cast on their merits and type. The actor that is cast is likely the best actor for the role. This is the category for which to strive. The dilemma is that there are many talented actors that are right for the same roles. It's the ones that properly market and promote themselves that separate themselves from the rest. They are the actors who usually get the jobs.

"An actor with little talent and good, solid marketing skills has a better chance of being cast than a talented actor with poor marketing skills. Learning to market yourself properly is the most valuable training an actor can have."
Bradford Hill, producer/director
Commercial Works, L.A.

Hang on, we will discuss getting your product to the proper distributors and retail outlets later. There are many things you will need to know and do before you are ready to take that step.

THE UNIONS

The entertainment industry is divided into several categories such as film, television, theater, television commercials, voice-over, and print advertising, as well as television and radio broadcasting, modeling, music, dance, etc. There are also both union and non-union productions and production companies.

Producers or production companies that sign contracts with unions are called *signatories*. Most non-union companies are not union signatories because of cost. Union productions cost more. For the professional actor that is starting out, non-union productions offer many excellent opportunities to learn, grow, and build a resume. However, in this industry, being a professional actor means belonging to a union. The catch is that it is difficult to get a union job unless you are a member of a union, and you can't join a union unless you work on a union job. The good news is that although it is difficult to get a union job, it's not impossible.

For our purposes, there are three labor unions to discuss.

SAG (Screen Actors Guild) represents actors and performers in film and television.

To qualify for SAG membership, an actor must meet one of the following conditions:

1. **Proof of SAG Employment:** Performers may join SAG upon proof of employment or prospective employment within two weeks or less by a SAG signatory company. Employment must be a principal or speaking role in a SAG project.

2. **Background Player Employment:** Performers may join SAG upon proof of employment as a SAG background player at full SAG rates and conditions for a minimum of three workdays subsequent to March 25, 1990. The employer must be signed to a SAG *Background Players Agreement*, and in a SAG project.

3. **Employment Under an Affiliated Performers' Union:** Performers may join SAG if they are a paid-up member of an affiliated performers' union (ACTRA, AEA, AFTRA, AGMA or AGVA) for a period of one year and have worked at least once as a principal performer in that union's jurisdiction.

For more information, contact SAG at **www.sag.org.**

AFTRA (American Federation of Television and Radio Artists) represents actors, performers, and broadcasters in television, radio, sound recordings, non-broadcast/industrial programming, and interactive programming. Any actor who has performed or intends to perform in AFTRA's jurisdiction is eligible for membership. Contact your Local office for specific information about AFTRA membership and its benefits. For more information, contact AFTRA at **www.aftra.org.**

AEA (Actors Equity Association) represents actors for theater and live performances. For membership requirements and general information, contact AEA at **www.actorsequity.org.**

These unions ensure fair, competitive wages and safe working conditions for professional actors and performers. Union membership will be necessary for your career to progress.

Presently, SAG and AFTRA are working towards consolidation. All members of SAG and AFTRA would then be represented by one labor union. This union consolidation has been tried in the past, but has failed. However, this time it looks like there may be ample support. For more information on union membership and/or the consolidation, contact your local office or log on to the sites listed above.

SCENE SIX
MARKETING TOOLS

THE 'ACTOR'S TOOL BELT'

For the professional actor, **marketing tools** are not only necessary tools, but tools of necessity. Many times, your marketing tools will be the industry's first impression of you and your product. Your marketing tools will help you generate exposure and create a demand for your product. Most importantly, your marketing tools will be a direct reflection of the professionalism that you, your business, and your product possess. Poor tools are a sign of an amateur. This is a relatively small industry and once you appear amateurish, it is difficult to recover. Instead of marketing yourself and creating exposure, you will be forced to do damage control—"Hey, remember me? I'm no longer an amateur!" You want to be professional. You want the best possible tools in your *'Actor's Tool Belt.'*

YOUR PICTURES

There are start up costs in creating your new business. Since, you are the product, and are trying to sell yourself, your pictures or **headshots** and your resumes will often be your first impression . . . make it a good one. Your brother, father or neighbor might have a camera—let them take pictures of sunsets. For headshots, hire a professional. Your picture and resume are the liaison between you and an agent, you and a manager, or you and a casting director.

> *"A great headshot gets an actor in the door. It's their business card. Their picture needs to tell a story and capture the attention of an agent or the person casting the role. A great picture has energy and a spark in the eyes."*
> **Charity Marquis, agent**
> **Osbrink Models & Talent, L.A.**

Think of your picture and resume as a print ad. Print ads are a valuable source of advertising. Thumb through your favorite magazine and take a look at the ads. The photos of the products advertised are not Polaroid's or snapshots. They are not pictures from a home PC or color photocopies. They are photos taken by professional photographers using the best light and state of the art techniques. Do not try to sell your product any other way.

"The shot has to reflect the actor who will walk in the door to audition. Of course, a photo of less than professional quality, no matter how much it looks like the performer, will not work."
Patty Grana-Miller, agent
The Bobby Ball Agency, L.A.

Choosing Your Photograper . . .

Choose your photographer carefully. Often, 'photographer' is another word for 'unemployed actor.' Hire a professional. Interview them first, and remember that you are the one doing the hiring. The personality of the photographer is so important. You and the photographer must be compatible. I strongly recommend that you set up appointments with several photographers to look at examples of their work. A photographer's *book* is a portfolio of his work. Their books will show samples of headshots, and reflect their individual style.

"Some people ask how I work. Half way through the first roll you will realize that I am your best friend for the day. We work together. My job as a photographer is to inspire you, to find your magic."
Dick Wieand, photographer
Dick Wieand Photography, L.A.

In the BOOK?

All professional photographers will have a book. Look at their work carefully. Does he or she specialize in men, women, or children? Is the bulk of their work fashion or commercial oriented? Do they understand lighting for ethnic actors? What kind of shots do they recommend for you? Do they shoot outdoors using natural light or in a studio? If you are not comfortable with the photographer, he/she will not be able to capture your appeal.

"The photographer's goal is to catch an honest moment. For example, if the subject smiles because he or she feels they are supposed to, it won't be organic. The thought has to be there first, then the photographer must catch it at the peak. After that it becomes imposed. Don't impose it! Just allow yourself to go wherever you want to be and let it happen."
Halstan Williams, photographer
Butch Williams Studios, Inc., L.A.

Your First Impression

How do you determine which photographers to interview? Ask questions. Ask other people in the business for recommendations. Ask agents, managers, acting coaches, etc. Probably the best source of information will be other actors. The most important question to ask another actor is, "is that picture getting you in the door?" Remember, your picture is the liaison between you and the industry. It's your business card. It's your first impression. Your picture is one of the most important tools that you have to market yourself. Don't skimp on your photographer. Take your time.

> *"Your picture must be a good representation of who you are. First, it must look like you and secondly, it must tell us who you are. It's important to remember that your picture is the first and most important marketing tool that you have. It has to be an honest, accurate representation of who you are as an actor."*
> **Bruce Economou, manager**
> **John Crosby Management, L.A.**

> *"Headshots must have a spark, something unique. Actors need to look like they are actually thinking."*
> **Richard DeLancy, manager**
> **DeLancy & Associates, L.A.**

Picture Formats and Styles

Industry standard for pictures is 8x10. Do not deviate from this standard. A *headshot* is from the neckline up. There is also what we call a *'3/4'* shot or *full-body shot*. A 3/4 or full-body shot enables a casting director to see body language and body type, which is particularly important for commercials and soaps.

> *"I prefer a shoulders up shot. I like the face to be close to life-sized but remain in the borders."*
> **Nancy Moon-Broadstreet, agent**
> **The Artists Group, LTD., L.A.**

AARON REVOIR   AGENT OR MANAGER

PHOTO BY: HALSTAN WILLIAMS

Michael Viruet   Agent or Manager

PHOTO BY: HALSTAN WILLIAMS

EXAMPLE:
8x10 Theatrical Headshot

"Stick to darker color clothes, nothing busy. Most important . . . wear clothes that do not wrinkle! The photographer may have you lean on one elbow on the ground and the shirt may wrinkle easily.

Material that lays on you like chenille or a light-weight cotton is ideal. Bring wardrobe that you can throw in your suitcase and when you pull it out, it is ready to wear. If you have a strong jawbone, you may want a large collar shirt to bring attention away, so it is not so prominent. If you have black hair, you may not want to wear a black shirt or blouse. A dark grey or blue color would be more ideal. If you are a child, you can go with a little bit lighter color than black but not white. Again, nothing busy."

Halstan Williams, photographer
Butch Williams Studios, Inc., L.A.

EXAMPLE:
8x10 Commercial Headshot

Picture Perfect!

Have your headshots taken dressed the way you will be type cast. Avoid extreme hairstyles. Kids should look like kids, not hookers or rock stars. Minors need only lip-gloss and mascara. Make a wardrobe list of what clothes to take with you to the photography session. This wardrobe should be comprised of flattering necklines and the appropriate apparel for your type. Think in terms of naturalness—no jewelry, natural make-up, and no busy plaids or prints. Discuss the look you want with the photographer. He or she will help to determine the type of wardrobe, and the number of changes you should bring. Since that's their area of expertise, let the photographer assist you.

> *"We prefer studio shots because they have cleaner, clearer backgrounds. I don't want to see bricks, a window, an arch, or a door. I just want to look into the eyes of the actor. Think about what sort of roles you want to be submitted for and take photos accordingly. You don't have to wear a stethoscope in the shot, but you can't have a bare midriff and low-rider jeans and expect to be (cast as) the head of pediatrics. Body shots are good if you're young and have a good one. No plaids, no prints, no dangly earrings, no distractions of any kind."*
> **Ginger Lawrence, agent**
> **A House of Representatives, L.A.**

> *" . . . adults will often find themselves 'reinventing' themselves— children and teens are just changing. I think adult actors should take pictures anytime they are trying to give a different image. Often an agent or manager will submit their client based on the breakdown using a specific picture that the client has provided. Children between the ages of six and up should do them every year to year and half."*
> **Todd J. Stein, manager**
> **Stein Entertainment Group, L.A.**

Casting directors will often call you in for an audition based upon a submitted picture. That's the image they want to see walk in for the interview. A casting director should immediately recognize you when you walk in the door. Often casting directors are matching up families or groups, so it's critical to them that you look like the picture submitted.

> *"It's crucial that the shot is representative of the talent. The actor must look like their headshot. Never over glamorize or take on a look that is unrealistic. Clothing and makeup should be clean and simple, so they don't distract from the talent. The shot should make the talent marketable by allowing casting directors and agents to see the talent fitting into a variety of roles."*
> **Charity Marquis, agent**
> **Osbrink Models & Talent, L.A.**

Keep your pictures current. I recommend getting new pictures every year. If you change your hairstyle or grow or shave your facial hair, you guessed it—***new pictures***.

> *"You need a new picture when your current picture isn't working anymore. That sounds cliché, but it's true. Maybe you've changed your look, hair, etc., and a new picture would help reflect these changes. Maybe the style of the clothes in the shot seem dated and it's time for a change. At the least, a new picture every two years is not unreasonable. Remember, it's your career; don't be afraid to invest in it."*
> **Bruce Economou, manager**
> **John Crosby Management, L.A.**

> *"An agent will determine when it's time for their client to get new pictures. If an actor isn't getting called in for auditions, their headshot may be holding them back. If they have changed their look, it's important to update their pictures. Young actors usually need to re-shoot more often as they mature."*
> **Charity Marquis, agent**
> **Osbrink Models & Talent, L.A.**

EXAMPLE:
8x10 Letter Box

Kathleen Gibson   AGENT OR MANAGER

PHOTO BY: DUKE TIRSHEL

Smile!

As you can see there are many types of pictures and headshots. Commercial agents will want upbeat, smiling, headshots or 3/4 shots. Pictures for a commercial agent should show a cute, funny look; a natural, smiling, comfortable look; or the actor as a young mom, businessman, etc. On the other hand, your theatrical agent may want a headshot that looks ***just like you***: a fun shot for sitcoms, a glamour shot for soaps, and an intense shot for film.

" . . . bring in samples of acceptable headshots that your agent likes to send out (indoor vs. outdoor, backgrounds and lighting), to show the photographer what you need."
Halstan Williams, photographer
Butch Williams Studios, Inc., L.A.

If you don't have a commercial or theatrical agent as yet, then only get a headshot or 3/4 shot that looks just like you. Once you have an agent, they will suggest what shots to get. After your photo session, your agent will want you to bring him/her your contact sheets or proofs, so they can pick out the ones they want to see blown up. Agents are the ones selling the image, so they must have input in your print advertising. If you have a manager, he or she will also assist you with your pictures.

"If the photograph makes you look better than you really are, you will disappoint everyone who brings you in because of it. If the photographs don't make you look as good as you do in real life, you won't get in the door."
Nancy Moon-Broadstreet, agent
The Artists Group, LTD., L.A.

Memories . . .
Commercial headshots tend to be fun and cute. Cute sells. Theatrical headshots are somewhat intense with more attitude: your greatest loss, your first love, your most nostalgic memory. When I look at a picture, I want to see that person with some degree of thought—something going on in their face and eyes, not just a smile or a frown. What I'm really looking for is attitude. One of the biggest advantages in our business is that all of the joys and disappointments in our lives can be used. Use these thoughts when you're having your picture taken. During your photo session, talk about the best or worst day of your life, the most embarrassing day, your first kiss, your first car, and your first —well, you've got the picture.

"A headshot needs to express your distinct look and personality while broadcasting the part of you that is most castable. If you have more than one look (blue-collar vs. white-collar / sexy vs. accessible), then each shot needs to fully express the key elements of that aspect of you without feeling like you are 'playing a role'."
Josh Schiowitz, agent
Schiowitz, Clay, Ankrum & Ross, Inc., L.A.

Try memorizing two monologues, and use them while you're being shot. One monologue should really touch you, and make you react. The other should be humorous, one that makes you giggle or laugh. Remember that working in front of a camera is reaction—acting is reacting. So the more memories you can re-experience during your photo shoot, the more genuine reactions and expressions we will see in your pictures. Prior to setting your appointment, prepare yourself to give your shots that something special.

> *"I love a picture that has the ability to tell a quick story. To make the actor have a personality is very important. The picture has to catch the something special in the person, whatever that may be—and let us see it."*
> **Todd J. Stein, manager**
> **Stein Entertainment Group, L.A.**

Black and White . . .

As a rule, headshots are in black and white. For theatrical use, I always recommend a photograph—a little more expensive than a lithograph, but worthwhile. For commercial use, a printed headshot (lithograph) can be used because of the volume of photos that are sent out. Before you make a choice on duplicating, go to a printer that does lithography and a lab that reproduces photographs to see samples of their work. Again, if you have representation, consult with your agent and/or manager.

Photographs are going to cost approximately $80-100 per hundred and $140-200 per two hundred. The lithograph, which is what a printed photo is called, is going to run $75-100 for the first 250, then $90-125 per five hundred of the same photo. The only time that I recommend color photos is if you have unusual coloring and that is part of your sell, such as a blue-eyed brunette or a green-eyed redhead. Full body or 3/4 color shots are not a bad idea if you have that special coloring.

You'll find a list of photography studios and photo duplication labs in the back of the book.

The Bottom Line

Prior to setting up your session appointment, it's important that you and the photographer are in agreement on the following:

→ How much time will he spend with you?
→ How many rolls of film will he be using?
→ How many changes of wardrobe will you be wearing?
→ What will you need to bring with you to the shoot?

→ Will there be a makeup and hair stylist?

→ What will the stylist charge?

→ Do you really need a stylist?

→ How long will it take to get your proofs or contact sheets?

→ How much time will it take to get your original prints back?

→ How many prints are included in the fee?

→ What's the cost of additional prints?

→ Does he handle any retouching, or will he recommend you to someone that does?

→ What are the retouching fees?

→ Who owns the negatives?

→ What are his guarantees? If you are not satisfied, will he do re-shoots?

→ Most importantly, what is the *bottom line cost?*

YOUR RESUME

If your picture is your print ad, then your *resume* is the ad copy. *Copy* is the text that tells the consumer about the product pictured. Your resume tells people that you're not just another pretty face. You may or may not have much experience to list, but your resume gives you the opportunity to show your training and special skills. Utilize this opportunity. The majority of industry professionals that I know will look at an actor's training first. Training tells us that you're *professional* and *prepared*.

Forget everything that you've learned about a resume in high school or college. The format of an actor's resume is different from the standard business resume. You do not list goals, career objectives, or references. Your work experience is not dated or listed in chronological order. I have included sample outlines—**follow them**.

Be Clear

Your resume should clearly state your name, union affiliation, representation, and contact information. If you're not a member of a union, put nothing. If you're eligible to join a union, most definitely put that. For example, if you have been a *Taft-Hartley* and have worked as a SAG actor, put SAG-Eligible.

Taft-Hartley is a federal law that makes it possible for non-union actors to work for a SAG signatory under a union contract. By working on a SAG project, you become '*SAG eligible';* this means you can work non-union or union before becoming a '*must join.*' Actors can work thirty days under a SAG signatory union contract. After thirty days, an actor must join in order to accept further union work. Again, contact your local SAG office for current rules, guidelines, and membership criteria. Contact SAG at **www.sag.org.**

When you are starting out, *SAG eligible* is a great place to be because you can audition for both union and non-union projects. Take the time to build a resume. Take advantage of all the non-union and student films that are available to you. Any type of on-camera experience will look good on your resume, and will help get you in the door.

Give Me A Call!

The contact numbers and information on your resume should be your agents, managers, or both. If you do not have representation, do not list your home phone number, home address, or social security number on your resume. I recommend setting up a separate phone line at home or using your cell phone number for your acting business. It is vitally important that your business line have voice mail or a **_reliable_** answering machine. You can also use an answering service or pager that has a voice mail feature. There are many unscrupulous characters in the entertainment industry and they don't need to have your home number, address, or social security number. Be smart and be safe. You don't want your personal information in the wrong hands.

Curriculum Vitae

Take a look at sample resumes. If you're on the West Coast, begin with film and TV roles. If you're on the East Coast, lead with your theater experience. The only stats that I think are necessary on a resume are eyes and hair. Weight fluctuates; and height might keep you from getting in the door (let's be realistic here). An adult actor's age should **_never_** appear on a resume. In fact, it is against the law to hire or discriminate against anyone based on age. You can be asked about your *age range* or whether or not you're a minor, but that's it. If you are a minor, it is common practice to list your date of birth (DOB).

Occasionally, you will be asked your age anyway, either directly or indirectly. I would discuss this with your manager or agent. It depends on how they are selling you. If you're *'eighteen to play younger,'* your manager or agent may want casting directors to know that up front. Let them handle the age range.

L.A. RESUME OUTLINE

NAME
UNIONS (SAG, AFTRA, AEA)

DOB (under 17):   **AGENCY or**
Hair: Eyes: **CONTACT #**

FILMS (Most recent project first)
"Name of Film"   Billing   Director and/or Production Co.
                        (Starring, Co-starring,
                        Support, Featured,)

TELEVISION (Most recent project first)
"Name of Show"   Prime-Time Billing   Producer and/or Production Co. or Network
(Episode Name)   (Starring, Guest-star, Co-starring, Featured)
                        Day Time Billing
                        (Contract Player, Recurring, Principle, U-5)

COMMERCIALS (Credits available upon request)

THEATER (Most recent production first)
"Name of Play"   Role Played   Theater/City and Director

TRAINING (Most recent workshop first)
Name of Teacher and/or School   List of skills acquired (Acting, Voice,   City
                                     Improv, Cold-Reading, Dance, etc.)

Education   Degrees   Majors

SPECIAL SKILLS
List any and all unique skills you have
(languages spoken, accents and dialects, sports, musical talents, impersonations, etc.)

NY RESUME OUTLINE

NAME
UNIONS (SAG, AFTRA, AEA)

DOB (under 17):   **AGENCY or**
Hair: Eyes: **CONTACT #**

THEATER (NY credits first-then regional and all other)
"Name of Play"   Role Played   Theater/City and Director

FILMS (Most recent project first)
"Name of Film"   Billing   Director and/or Production Co.
                      (Starring, Co-starring,
                      Support, Featured,)

TELEVISION (Most recent project first)
"Name of Show"   Prime-Time Billing   Producer and/or Production Co. or Network
(Episode Name)   (Starring, Guest-star, Co-starring, Featured)
                      Day Time Billing
                      (Contract Player, Recurring, Principle, U-5)

COMMERCIALS (Credits available upon request)

TRAINING (Most recent workshop first)
Name of Teacher and/or School   List of skills acquired (Acting, Voice,   City
                                     Improv, Cold-Reading, Dance, etc.)

Education   Degrees   Majors

SPECIAL SKILLS
List any and all unique skills you have
(languages spoken, accents and dialects, sports, musical talents, impersonations, etc.)

Catch The Train . . .

I believe your training is the most important part of the resume—where you've studied: with whom; and for how long, especially if you are light on film and TV experience. If you're going to have surgery, you want to know that the surgeon is well trained. Training gives you credibility; and as I've said, training is a sign of a professional.

> *Training " . . . shows that the actor takes his/her work seriously, but I look at the whole package on a resume."*
> **Rosemary Welden, CSA, casting director**
> **L.A.**

Training tells me that the actor is ready to begin his career. Where you've trained is also important. Professional training is a plus. To have recognizable names on your resume under training is a benefit, whether it be a professional conservatory, a well-known acting coach, or a university known for its television, film, and theater departments.

> *"For the young folks that don't have much experience, I definitely look for training. A good school or conservatory holds a lot of weight. The more experienced actor—where was that experience? Good regional theaters are impressive. Who were the directors? If you've done film or television work, what was your character, who directed, were you a principal, co-star, guest-star, or under 5?"*
> **Breanna Benjamin, casting director**
> **Breanna Benjamin Casting, N.Y.**

All your training is important on your resume. Include your teachers for voice, diction, dialects, dance, movement, etc. It's a small community. Their names may be recognizable and carry some weight.

> *"I like to see a well rounded resume from an actor. I always tell actors that when writing their resume, 'Every picture tells a story.' They should be honest and concise. Film/television. I look for theater. Where has the actor studied. Who has the actor studied with and is he/she currently active with a teacher or class. If there is no film/television yet . . . type in the words and leave it blank. **Everyone has to start somewhere and I***

always leave it to the laws of physics . . . if there is an empty space, something will arrive to fill the void."
Linda Phillips-Palo, CSA, casting director
Phillips/McGee Casting, L.A.

"All The World's a Stage . . ."

Theater experience and training is also important on a resume, especially if an actor is light on TV and film experience. A theater background tells me that this actor has maintained a role on stage for two hours. So, I am certainly confident that he or she can handle one minute of dialogue for camera. Theater experience is very important and it helps you as an actor. Theatre gives you the confidence to be in front of an audience, and remember, every time you audition, you have an audience. Take advantage of every opportunity to audition for theater, whether it be high school, college, or community theater. If you're in L.A., audition for Equity Waiver theater productions, and in N.Y., audition for showcase and off-off Broadway theater productions. The more experience, the better.

"I like it when an actor has theater credits, I think stage is an important training ground."
Stanzi Stokes, CSA, casting director
Stanzi Stokes Casting, L.A.

"The one thing that bugs me is when people list plays they have been in, and then only say whether they had a lead or 'co-star' role. For those of us who know theater, we want to know if you played Juliet or Lady Capulet, Willy Loman or Biff."
Josh Schiowitz, agent
Schiowitz, Clay, Ankrum & Ross, Inc., L.A.

Giddie Up!

Hobbies, skills, or things you enjoy doing, such as skateboarding or dancing, may be assets on your resume. If you list swimming as a skill, you need not be an Olympic swimmer, but you do have to be able to swim well for an extended period of time. If you list horseback riding as a skill, you better be sure that you can stay on and stop the horse when you need to. Don't laugh! I've seen actors that claim to be proficient with horses ride right into a camera crew. Producers are more careful today, and will often take the actors out to actually see them ride first.

Being a computer wiz, a court stenographer, or even a bartender, requires valuable skills. Knowing how to wait tables is a skill. There is a correct way to hold a tray and to take an order, and virtually every film or TV show has some sort of restaurant scene. Often your day job and hobbies will become valuable skills in your acting career.

> *"I think special skills (and there is mixed opinion on this) are interesting. Especially if the actor is just starting out . . . because* **_cleverly listed and accurate special skills encourage dialogue_**. *Also, if I'm looking for a court reporter or someone who can handle a weapon, that knowledge is helpful in narrowing down the field."*
> **Linda Phillips-Palo, CSA, casting director**
> **Phillips/McGee Casting, L.A.**

Tennis Anyone?

Special skills are so important on a resume. If a casting director is casting a scene that requires actors to interact while playing tennis, the casting director will look for tennis skills on the resumes submitted. We simply do not have the time to teach an actor how to play tennis for the shoot, unless of course we are talking about the star. If a special skill is required for a star, they would be allowed months to acquire that skill. Be sure to include special skills on your resume. Your skills could get you in the door.

> *"I don't want to see extra work listed on a resume. I don't want to see objectives or a mission statement. I don't want to see that you have bartending, catering, or construction experience. I want to hire an actor. I know that you probably have a day job, but don't remind me."*
> **Breanna Benjamin, casting director**
> **Breanna Benjamin Casting, N.Y.**

At Your Request . . .

Notice that it says on the sample resume under *Commercials*, 'Credits Upon Request.' Theatrical casting directors and directors don't need to be aware of the commercials you have done. We don't need the specifics. 'Credits Upon Request' tells me that you have worked in front of the camera. So if you have theater experience, good training, and I feel that you have had some commercial experience in front of the camera, I am more likely to call you in for an audition.

Should a commercial agent or commercial casting director ask for credits, they're usually asking for your *'conflicts.'* If you're auditioning for a Ford commercial, they want to be sure that you don't have a Chevrolet spot currently airing. This is the time to tell them of your commercial experience, and if you have no commercial experience when asked, you say "none." Be honest.

8 x 10 = ?

Standard size for both pictures and resumes is 8x10. Your resume should be **stapled** to the back of your picture, same side up. **Staple** your resume. Do not glue, tape, or bubble gum your pictures and resumes together. Besides being industry standard, staples make it easy to update your pictures with current resumes. Casting directors and their assistants comb through hundreds of submissions a day. Should your resume become separated from your picture, one or the other will certainly wind up in the 'circular file,' ***the trash***.

Your resume should have at least three staples, two at the top and one at the bottom to insure that the resume does not separate from the photo. Your resume should be updated and current. Each time you are cast or complete any additional training, add it. Print new updated resumes. Do not use a pen, pencil, marker, crayon, or spray paint to update your resume. Take the time and do it right.

ASSIGNMENT #1:
Using the templates in this chapter, create your own resume.

THE DEMO TAPE

Most agents and managers will ask if you have 'tape on yourself,' or a ***demo reel.*** Along with your picture and resume, a **good** ***demo reel***, or ***demo tape***, is your next best marketing tool. I emphasize 'good' because a poor reel will hurt you more than help you. A demo reel is a compilation or montage of your best work. A reel would consist of various scenes or partial scenes, from any films, TV shows, or commercials that you have done. Your reel should show your range of talent and looks as an actor.

Although many actors are now using DVD or CD-ROM formats, VHS is still the industry standard for an actor's demo reel. Often, several people will look at actors' reels at the same time. It's difficult for a number of people to huddle around a computer monitor to view a CD-ROM, and the full screen resolution will likely be poor. As far as DVD formats go, not all casting facilities or production offices are equipped with such equipment, yet. I suggest you ask your agent or manager which format they would prefer that you have ready to hand out.

Theatrical casting directors, directors, and producers don't want to see commercials and vice versa. As you start to accumulate a body of work, you will need to have two separate reels. You will need a *commercial reel* and a *theatrical reel.*

I will say it again: a poor reel will hurt you more than it will help you. Having no reel is better than having a bad one. The quality of the clips that you use in your reel must be top notch. The sound must be crisp and clear; and although many of us now have some sort of video editing software on our PCs, I urge you to have your reel professionally done.

> *"A good reel is well organized and short (three to five minutes). It showcases the best of the actor's work. I like something that I can cue up to show my director. The best reels have the actor's name, picture and phone number on the case and on the reel spine, in case the two get separated. The tape itself should have a picture, actor's name and agent or phone number. If available, a montage of looks from actual work in television and film, and then some good dramatic and comedic scenes that show variety and versatility."*
> **Linda Phillips-Palo, CSA, casting director**
> **Phillips/McGee Casting, L.A.**

"To Be or Not To . . ."

Your reel should show your best work. It should be properly and professionally labeled with your current contact information and be no longer than five minutes in length. Like pictures, you should seek the advice and opinions of those in the industry when it comes to determining the quality of the clips you wish to use, as well as the finished product. Your mother gave you a standing ovation when you sang out of key during your sixth grade talent show. You should avoid the opinions of family and friends. You need honest, constructive, and knowledgeable feedback. If you have representation, seek the advice of your agent and/or manager. If you don't have representation, seek the opinions of your acting coaches or instructors. They will be able to give you some solid advice.

> *I look for "A good cross-section of work. Recent work that represents what the actor looks like now. Film and television work only. Separate reels for theatrical and commercial work. I don't want to see stage work or monologues on a reel. If you're forty, I don't want to see what you did when you were seventeen."*
> **Breanna Benjamin, casting director**
> **Breanna Benjamin Casting, N.Y.**

" . . . a reel should simply highlight work. Don't put a ten-minute scene on a reel no matter how good you think you were/are. The purpose of an actors reel is to showcase a variety of work."
Linda Phillips-Palo, CSA, casting director
Phillips/McGee Casting, L.A.

Most producers know the importance of a professional actor's reel and will likely be accommodating when it comes to giving actors copies of commercials. But, you have to ask. Acquiring scenes from TV shows and feature films will be more difficult, but not impossible. There is a certain amount of secrecy when it comes to films. It is often impossible to get any kind of clip prior to a film's release, and because most productions disband once a film is completed, it can be difficult tracking down the proper people. However, it's not impossible, so keep trying.

Many actors have to resort to their VCRs to get tape of any commercials or TV programs in which they have appeared. They will often ask everyone they know to set their VCRs, as well. If more than one person tries to tape a show, there is a much better chance of getting a clean copy. I own three VCRs, and can't operate one of them. Films eventually make their way to cable, which gives actors another opportunity to get tape on him/herself. A lot of actors find it difficult to tape scenes from videos or DVDs because most are now equipped with anti-piracy devices.

Air Checks . . .

There are companies that do *'air checks'* for actors. This means, at an actor's request, they will copy any TV show or movie that appears on TV, and it will be broadcast quality. Actors just need to alert them with the day, date, and time that the show or film will air; they'll do the rest. When actors have to wait until a film comes out in video to obtain a copy of their scenes, they take the tapes or DVDs to professionals to *'lift'* their scenes. A lift means that they cut relevant scenes and put them on a demo tape. Refer to the back of the book for video demo editing and production studio recommendations. Many of these studios provide air checks, as well.

Note: Look into the laws concerning the copying and/or duplication of licensed and/or copyrighted material with and without written consent, consult with an attorney, or do so at your own risk.

Student Films and Shorts:

Starting out, it may be easier to build your demo reel with student films or shorts. These are films that students from universities such as AFI, BSU, UCLA, USC, and NYU produce as a sample of their work. They hold auditions and go through the same process that professional film projects do. You, as an actor, don't get paid, but you do get a video copy of the film to use for your demo reel. Providing they are legitimate student films from accredited universities, these films are *'SAG waivers'* and are often quite good. It's a win-win situation for everyone. They need actors for their demo and you need a demo tape. If the film is sold, you will profit. But the films are usually used to showcase the work of the directors, writers, cinematographers, editors, etc. Hopefully, the director and producer will eventually land a paying project, remember how talented and cooperative you were, and want to work with you again.

Director Labs:
The Directors Guild of America (DGA) offers members workshop opportunities to direct scenes. Members can try out new material and keep their skills sharp. The DGA lab has a casting director for their lab films and directing workshops. Contact the DGA for submission information. Let your agent and/or manager know that you are interested in DGA projects so that they can submit you, as well. This is a great way to gain exposure and get tape on yourself. Contact the DGA at **www.dga.org.**

Fox Searchlight offers a film lab for new directors. They also have their own casting directors. Let your agent and/or manager know that you are interested in the *Searchlight Lab* projects so they can submit you as well. This is great exposure; you can build a reel and work on the Fox lot. Contact Fox Searchlight at **www.foxsearchlight.com.**

Do it Yourself . . .
You can also hire a studio and a director to shoot a scene for you to use as a demo. Don't use workshop or classroom tape. If you and your scene partner invest in a studio and director that knows what they're doing, you could get a decent demo tape. Be careful. Ask around for any referrals and make sure you see sample tapes before you make any decisions or write any checks. This is a costly way to go. I vote for the student film.

> I "do not recommend self-produced demo reels. Actors should make video copies of every TV and film piece the actor's been in, no matter how small the part. It's better to see the actor in a small professional scene than any self-produced video."
> **Laya Gelff, agent**
> **Laya Gelff Agency, L.A.**

"I don't mind the self-made demo reel if it is professionally done."
Barry Freed, agent
Barry Freed Company, L.A.

"Actor produced demo reels can work, but if they look like 'actor produced' demo reels they do not serve much purpose. The main reason for this sort of reel is to show off your acting chops. If you can do that without making it look like an amateur put it together then it certainly can work, at least in finding a good agent. People have gotten auditions and ultimately jobs by putting themselves on tape, so a well produced reel can do the same. Just remember the demo reel is like a trailer for a movie called ___(insert your name)."
Josh Schiowitz, agent
Schiowitz, Clay, Ankrum & Ross, Inc., L.A.

THE VOICE DEMO

A *voice demo* is a sample of your voice-over work: TV voice-overs, radio commercials and animation voices. Take your produced work to a sound editor, have him lift your work, and cut a voice demo for you. If you have little or no experience, you can hire a voice-over director and go into a sound studio to record and cut your demo. Another costly venture, but if you get a good demo, it will pay for itself. It's impossible to acquire voice-over representation without a good voice demo. Many actors still use cassette tapes, however CDs are less expensive and are becoming industry standard. If you have representation, ask your agent and/or manager which format they prefer.

Prior to cutting a voice-over demo, I suggest you sign up for a voice-over class taught by a studio professional. You will probably find that the teacher will also be able to assist you with the production of your tape. Picking the right copy for your voice and the right music to go under the copy takes a pro. They're expensive, but you get what you pay for.

Refer to the back of the book for voice-over classes and voice-over studios that produce and/or edit actor voice demos.

THE PORTFOLIO

A *portfolio* is used for the commercial print actor/model to keep tear sheets from commercial print jobs. This is your picture resume of commercial shots that show you in different settings: washing your car, playing with your children, splashing in a pool, studying in school, and/or sitting in an office. You'll need a commercial print portfolio to obtain a commercial print agent. Commercial print agents represent talent for print ads, billboards, point of purchase, and brochures.

The portfolio warrants mention, however it is not a primary focus in this book. Commercial print is certainly something I would recommend an actor explore. It offers an actor one more career avenue, and another opportunity to make money.

When discussing a commercial headshot with your photographer, ask if he also shoots for commercial print. Commercial print pictures will need to be color, as you will want them for a commercial print composite, *comp card*, or *Zed Card*.

The *Zed Card* was named after the originator of the print model's composite card, Sebastian Zed. He is married to Dorthee Parker, a major modeling agent. The Parker-Zed Agency, in Germany, was the first agency to use the Zed Card.

SCENE SEVEN
PRODUCT DISTRIBUTION

THE DISTRIBUTORS

Selling lemonade to passersby on a hot summer day can be quite rewarding for a child. Doing your best 'Dirty Harry' impression in the shower can be rewarding, as well. Taking your talents to the next level is the hard part. You want your lemonade in every kitchen in the country. You want your face on every TV. That's where the distributors come in.

The distributors for your product are the personal managers, commercial and theatrical agents.

AGENTS

There are theatrical agents and commercial agents. You will likely have the need for both. As you seek representation, ***avoid any agent that is not union franchised***. Only union franchised agents can represent union actors and submit on union projects. If you want to further your career, you must sign with a franchised agent.

Being franchised by a particular union means that the agent must adhere to the rules and guidelines set by those unions. SAG and AFTRA franchised agents can only charge ten percent commission for any acting job that you book. AEA franchised agents charge a commission based on the role and theater contract. They have a tier commission structure that changes regularly. For more information: **www.actorsequity.org.**

No reputable agent will charge you any additional fees, demand that you take classes from a certain teacher, or have your pictures taken by a certain photographer. A reputable agent will have favorites and make suggestions, not demands. If you are asked for a fee, ***run***, don't walk.

> *"When you're just starting out, a good, solid agent is all you really need. If you are a new, fresh face, it shouldn't be that hard for an agent to get you in a room with a casting director. From there, it's up to you."*
> **Bruce Economou, manager**
> **John Crosby Management, L.A.**

Theatrical agents represent actors for daytime and primetime TV, which consists of sitcoms, soaps, episodic, movies made for television and cable, miniseries, and pilots. They also represent actors for feature films as well as theater. Some SAG and AEA franchised theatrical agents also represent dancers as well as singers. Theatrical agents will be SAG, AFTRA and AEA franchised, and will be licensed by the state.

Commercial agents represent actors for on-camera commercials, infomercials, music videos, and industrial films, as well as voice-over and commercial print, in most cases. A voice-over agent will represent clients for voice-over TV commercials, radio commercials, narratives, multi-media, animation, or any project where you hear the voice but do not see the talent speaking. Voice-over is 'voice over image.' Most agencies have a commercial print department for print work and still photography. Again, this is another area that actors should pursue, as commercial print agents are seeking 'real people,' not models. Some larger commercial agencies will have a song and dance department as well, since many commercials use singers and dancers. Commercial agents will be SAG and AFTRA franchised, and will also be licensed by the state.

Commercial agencies represent more actors at any given time than theatrical agencies. On average, a commercial agency may represent one to three hundred actors, depending on the size of the agency. Theatrical agencies represent fewer clients than commercial agencies, averaging about fifty to a hundred actors, depending on the size of the agency. A commercial agent might submit six to ten people per role; a theatrical agent may only submit one.

Commercial agents need a larger roster because they can submit more clients per role than a theatrical agent. Often, commercial casting directors are more interested in a look, and therefore, if your resume is light and you're starting out, it is easier to obtain commercial representation based upon your look. By submitting headshots to commercial agents, you are more likely to get an interview than with a theatrical agent.

> *"The number one thing I look for in a potential client is the proper mix of talent and castability."*
> **Josh Schiowitz, agent**
> **Schiowitz, Clay, Ankrum & Ross, Inc., L.A.**

Theatrical agents don't like to create a conflict within their own stable of people. A theatrical agent would not want to take on an actor who is similar in *type* to an existing client, whereas a commercial agent could have 'like' types. Commercial talent is a separate expertise from acting. ***Not all actors can sell soap and not all commercial talent can act.***

Commercials, more often than not, require a particular 'look.' Commercial agents are selling *looks* or types, and are always looking for new commercial talent to add to their rosters. This is why I always recommend that an actor go for commercial representation first.

"Sometimes a 'look' and an 'attitude' holds more weight in L.A. than it does in N.Y. There's no 'smoke and mirrors' or 'retakes' in theatre, so you have to know your stuff. Pretty is not enough in theatre. A pretty or handsome person with minimum acting training or talent may be able to pull off certain film or TV roles, but you won't see them on Broadway."
Breanna Benjamin, casting director
Breanna Benjamin Casting, N.Y.

A list of franchised agents is available through the **ATA** (Association of Talent Agents), as well as the offices of SAG, AFTRA and AEA. Agent directories are listed in the back of this book.

PERSONAL MANAGERS

I am often asked the difference between a personal manager and an agent. <u>**A manager is like a marriage, while an agent is more like a relationship.**</u> A manager will groom you and assist you in *creating your image.* As I like to say, they will hand hold. An agent *distributes your image* to casting directors. An agent is the salesman; he/she will go over the breakdowns every morning and distribute headshots and resumes accordingly. An agent's job is to get you that interview, negotiate your deal, and sign the contract.

A manager will " . . . guide the actor in all his/her career decisions, and . . . help the agents market their client. The manager is important at every level of an actor's career. It's important to have a team, a team that works together from the very start. That way it's a journey and it's one done with a solid foundation."
Todd J. Stein, manager
Stein Entertainment Group, L.A.

When parents act as their child's manager, it " . . . usually doesn't work in the best interest of the child. We (agents and managers) have chosen this field for a reason. I love the kids and want to look out for them professionally and personally. I know what's out there, the good and the bad. Some parents are not going to recognize the difference, or know how to handle various situations. Also, usually, kids don't want to listen

to their parents. If there is an agent and/or manager involved, the children tend to listen to us and we can get them going and psyched to push forward."
Carolyn Thompson-Goldstein, agent
Amsel Eisenstadt & Frazier, Inc., L.A.

Managers have smaller client lists, and are in a better position to spearhead your career. A manager will look at the overall picture and see where you will be in five years. They are long-term growth relationships. A manager may manage ten to fifteen clients, while a theatrical agent at a particular agency may represent fifty clients. Therefore, a manager has much more time to do follow-up. Managers, unlike agents, are not union franchised and are not regulated by the state. Therefore, managers are not limited as far as commissions are concerned, but usually charge between 10 and 20 percent.

"SAG franchised agents get 10 percent. Managers can charge 10 to 20 percent but most charge 15 percent. Agents can negotiate, managers can not. Agents can procure work for their clients. Managers are not suppose to procure (or solicit) work for their clients. They are to offer counsel and guidance."
Bruce Economou, manager
John Crosby Management, L.A.

"Most of our clients have managers, mostly because most of our clients come to us from managers. It's a huge expense, but because there is so much competition today, it does give you a competitive edge. But there are managers and there are __managers__. Make certain you're with one who is really working for you and doesn't already have three of you on his client list."
Ginger Lawrence, agent
A House of Representatives, L.A.

Managers are usually more receptive to signing a ***development client*** (new to market) than an agent. A manager will usually ask for a three to five year contract, because it takes at least that long to develop a new-to-market actor. In all fairness to the manager, they need that time to groom you and assist you with the networking process. It may take time for you to start making money, and in the meantime, the manager is getting 10 to 20 percent of nothing.

Do I Need a Manager?

When should an actor consider a manager? I'm asked this question all the time.

"An actor should consider having a manager when he/she feels they are not auditioning enough or realize their agent needs help."
Barry Freed, agent
Barry Freed Company, L.A.

An actor should consider a manager "When there's something to manage."
Nancy Moon-Broadstreet, agent
The Artists Group, LTD., L.A.

"What do you need a manager for if there isn't anything to manage? Their contracts are iron clad, and an actor can tie themselves up for years, even if they are unhappy and want out."
Vaughn D. Hart, agent
Vaughn D. Hart & Associates, L.A.

I "do not recommend a manager for an actor in the early career stages. There's plenty of time to get a manager once the actor is established."
Laya Gelff, agent
Laya Gelff Agency, L.A.

At one point, the thinking was that you really didn't need a manager until you started making at least fifty thousand dollars a year because you didn't have a career to manage. Today, managers not only manage careers, they develop careers. If you find a legitimate manager who is excited about you and believes in your talent, then that's the time to consider a manager!

"When an actor starts to take off, career decisions have to be made. It can be very helpful to have a manager on your team to help counsel and guide you as you move to the next level."
Bruce Economou, manager
John Crosby Management, L.A.

"Many parents act as their child's manager. If they have any knowledge of the business, and see that the child gets trained and coached properly, they can do a good job."
Judy Savage, agent
The Savage Agency, L.A.

Another thing a good manager should be able to do is to assist you with finding the agent that is just right for you. Your agent must be compatible with your manager; together they will form your team.

A list of managers can be found through the **Talent Managers Association** (TMA), as well as the personal manager directories listed in the back of this book. Contact TMA at **www.talentmanagers.org.**

ABC's . . .

As an actor's career progresses, he may move from a *'C' agent* on up to an *'A' agent*, but will often retain the same personal manager. Often, a major agency will not look at a new-comer, and will leave it to a smaller boutique agency to establish a name for that newcomer. Naturally, a move after you've become established seems unfair to the agent that built your career. Unfortunately, this is business, and as an actor becomes known, it is better business for them to join a 'packaging agency.'

A *packaging agency* represents directors, writers, producers, stars, and series regulars. Packaging means the agency will submit their clients from a variety of trades for a particular project. They are able to package projects with their own clients and sell the entire package to a studio. For example, a package may include a script, star, and director. When an agency packages a project, it also gives them more leverage when submitting talent for supporting roles.

The Nature of the Business

There seems to be little loyalty in our business, and I have always applauded the actors who have stayed with the manager and agent who made them a star. However, it's the larger agencies that can package, promote, and demand the big bucks.

TARGETING THE RIGHT AGENT AND MANAGER

The entertainment industry is divided into ***commercial*** and ***theatrical***. There are commercial and theatrical agents, commercial and theatrical casting directors, directors, producers and crews. Again, it's important that you eventually seek representation in both areas.

There's been a major shift in the business, and many theatrical agencies that never represented commercially now have commercial departments, and many commercial agencies now have theatrical departments. Some agencies will ask you to sign with them 'across the board,' meaning they will represent you commercially and theatrically. But more often than not, an agency will sign you commercially, but not theatrically, when you're starting out.

> *"Any actor seeking representation should always sense that the agent in question has a great desire to represent him. He should never try to sell his way into the office. An actor should always check out the agent's background and reputation. Some agents are better for certain types of actors and not others."*
> **Barry Freed, agent**
> **Barry Freed Company, L.A.**

Coast to Coast . . .

The West Coast works on ***exclusive contracts***, meaning that you can only sign with one theatrical and one commercial agent, while the East Coast works on a ***non-exclusive*** basis. On the East Coast, you may register with more than one agency theatrically and commercially, although there are some East Coast agents who want that exclusive agreement. It is easier to function as an ***independent***, not signed with a particular agent, on the East Coast. Some larger agencies have offices on both coasts. However, just because you are signed with a particular agency on the West Coast does not mean that their office on the East Coast will represent you as well. Agents work independently of each other. Don't be misled and presume that if you sign on one coast, you are automatically represented on the other.

ASSIGNMENT #2:

Buy two spiral notebooks. Put one of them on your television set. Carry the other one with you at all times. You'll be creating a database for your personal marketing campaign by beginning to identify and research the people you need to know in the entertainment industry. The first category being agents.

Who's Your Agent?

How do you find the right agent? There are a number of ways. The best source of information is word of mouth. Your acting coaches and teachers are a great source of information. Those that teach tend to have been in this industry a long time. They will have their own personal experiences as well as the experiences of their many students. Ask questions! What agents do they recommend for you? Does your acting coach produce showcases, and if so, which agents attend regularly? Keep track of the information you gather in your notebook.

> *"First, look for the right agent for you, not just an agent. This involves a little homework on the actor's part and some intuition that each party 'speaks the same language' and has a good affinity for each other."*
> **Patty Grana-Miller, agent**
> **The Bobby Ball Agency, L.A.**

Trade publications such as *Back Stage West* (West Coast), *Back Stage* (East Coast), and the *Hollywood Reporter* offer interviews and articles about agents and agencies, as well as give background on what they did prior to their present position. You'll find promotion announcements, career changes and career moves. Add this information to your notebook.

I would also suggest going to showcase theaters in New York, Equity Waiver theaters in L.A., or any theater productions in your hometown. I find that there's usually at least one actor that will give a performance that makes an evening worthwhile, even if the overall production is weak. I've seen a lot of very good theater productions and have very seldom been disappointed. There seems to always be that one actor who stands out. After the curtain falls, go backstage and ask that actor whose performance impressed you, who his agent and/or manager is. Now, I have never met an actor who didn't enjoy talking about him/herself, so they'll be happy to tell you. Write the names down in your notebook.

Wherever or whenever you meet a fellow actor, ask them about their representation. Ask questions about their agents and managers and keep track of the information in your notebook. While you're on an audition, check the sign-in sheet. Which agents are listed more frequently? Make note of them in your notebook.

Unfortunately, many actors tear down their agents. Having been an agent myself, I know that being an agent is the most thankless job there is. So, no matter what actors may say about their agents, the fact is, they are signed with them, so there has to be some redeeming quality.

"Can I Help You?"

Another way of finding information on agents, which is time consuming but worthwhile, is to simply watch your favorite TV shows—thus, the reason for keeping a notebook on your TV. The actor that says, "Can I help you?" or "This way please" is a *day player*. It takes a hard working agent to get an actor on a top show. Watch the end credits for the actor's name and then look the actor up in the *Academy Player's Directory*. The *Academy Player's Directory*, or *New York's Player's Guide*, will give you the agent's name. Keep track of this information in your notebook. You can also obtain this and other information at **www.imdb.com.** The Player's Directory: **www.playersdirectory.com.** New York's Player's Guide: **www.playersguideny.com.**

The Award Goes To . . .

Often, on awards shows, winners will acknowledge and thank their agents and/or managers. Actors will often acknowledge their agents and/or managers during interviews on entertainment shows or in trade publications. If an actor takes the time to acknowledge or thank their agent and/or manger, they must be worth thanking. Now that you're in business for yourself, it will pay to be inventive in the ways you gather information. As far as this industry goes, Hollywood and New York City are small towns, and information is readily available. However you get it, keep track of your information in your notebook.

"Don't Squeeze the Charmin"

Asking actors about their commercial agents or encouraging actors to relate their commercial audition history are great ways to acquire information about commercial agents. Word of mouth will always be your best resource. **You can also log onto www.ecreativesearch.com to track down the names of the talent in particular commercials.** You can then find the name of their commercial agent through SAG or the *Academy Players Directory*. Any commercial agent will be dually impressed by your research.

After awhile, you will hear certain names more often than others. You will begin to get an idea of the agents who are worth pursuing. Now you must target the right ones for you.

EXERCISE #4

Go through all of the notes you've made on agents and managers. Weigh all of the opinions, both good and bad. Which agents work hard for your type? Which agents work hard for talent with your experience? Which managers work hard for your type? Which managers are good development managers?

Using the worksheets in the back of the book, target your top five choices for theatrical agents, your top five choices for commercial agents, and your top five choices for managers. This information will be used later to create your *database*.

SCENE EIGHT
THE BUYERS

CASTING DIRECTORS

Casting directors are independent contractors or employees that are hired by studios, networks, and production companies to cast films, MOWs (movies of the week), TV shows, pilots, sitcoms, soaps, commercials, industrials, music videos, etc. Good casting directors are worth their weight in gold. Casting directors are hired for their vast knowledge of the talent pool and their working relationships with agents and managers.

Casting directors, as we have discussed, are the *buyers*. They are not buyers in the sense that they write the checks, or even make the final decisions, for that matter. Casting directors follow trends and keep track of the available talent pool, both new and established. They make recommendations as to the most talented and the most recognizable name actors available for a given role, based on the allowable budget. A buyer employed by a retail-clothing store will follow fashion trends and seek out the highest quality garments within their budget. A buyer's budget is based on the retail store's demographics. A buyer for Sears isn't going to recommend the store stock $6,000 gowns. Likewise, a casting director isn't going to recommend an actor like Tom Cruise for a sitcom because he is far too expensive.

There are several types of casting directors. There are *theatrical casting directors* and *commercial casting directors*. Some theatrical casting directors are considered *television casting directors*. *Feature casting directors* also are typed 'mainstream' or 'low-budget.' By mainstream, I am referring to big-budget studio films that are released in theaters nationwide, or worldwide. Low-budget films will typically have a budget under two million dollars, and are usually released on cable and/or video. Check your CD directories to find out a casting director's expertise or specialization. **You can also obtain a list of theatrical casting directors through CSA, *Casting Society of America*, or www.imdb.com. CSA: www.castingsociety. com.** Refer to the back of the book for a list of CD directories.

Theatrical casting directors cast for feature films, sitcoms, soaps, episodic, miniseries and MOWs. Theatrical casting directors determine who is brought in for the first read, pre-screens, and sets up the callback readings for the director and, eventually, for the producers. The casting director will also make offers and negotiate with the actors' agents, as well as prepare the *deal memos* (agreements for contracts).

Commercial casting directors cast *on-camera* (OC) commercials that are aired regionally and nationally, as well as *'made and played in'* spots for local markets. A made and played in spot, for example, would be a commercial that is shot in Arizona and only aired only in Arizona. Some commercial casting directors also do *voice-over* (VO) casting.

Commercial casting directors also cast *industrials* (non-air training films) and radio spots. The commercial casting director determines who comes in to audition and who is video-taped. The video is then sent to the client and production company for review. The casting director will schedule callbacks, make offers to commercial agents, and handle contracts.

You can obtain a list of commercial casting directors through CCDA, *Commercial Casting Directors of America* or any CD directory. CCDA: (323) 722-8012.

Background/Extra casting agencies or services list non-speaking background actors or *'extras'* as they are commonly referred to. Theatrical and commercial casting directors cast principle roles (speaking roles) only. They do not handle extras. A production company will deal directly with an extra casting agency or service when casting background talent.

Extra casting agencies or services represent background actors for a fee. As an actor, you can list with as many of these agencies as you choose, as long as you pay the fee for each one. These agencies usually charge a one-time listing fee of fifteen to sixty dollars. They list both union and non-union actors. *Only extra casting services* can legally charge a fee for representation. SAG, AFTRA or AEA franchised agencies cannot charge a fee to represent you; they can only charge you a commission.

I have listed a few of the larger extra casting agencies in the back of this book. A more complete list can be found in directories like, *The Working Actors Guide*.

RESEARCHING CASTING DIRECTORS

As you read this, think of the last movie you saw. What was the name of the film? Who was the director? Who produced it? Who *cast* it? It's okay if you don't remember the names; few people do. However, it is important that you start keeping track of this information from now on. The next time you go to a movie, bring your notebook and write down information. Take notes. At the end of the movie, write down something about the casting. Were the characters believable? Did the actors draw you into the story? Did you get involved? These are all elements of good casting.

Often, the stars of a film come packaged with the project. So, you need to write down your comments on the supporting cast. In the film *Jerry Maguire*, for example: Tom Cruise was a perfect *Jerry Maguire*, but I believe he came with the project or there would have been no movie. However, the supporting cast was also marvelous. It was the supporting cast that endeared us to *Jerry Maguire* even more. **A fantastic site for film research is www.imdb.com.**

It Worked for Me

After you see a film, ask yourself: Did the story line work? Was the film well cast? What was the one thing about the film that you really liked? This is information you are gathering for your cover letters, so you will have something interesting to say to the casting directors, directors, and producers, when you prepare your mailings in the following chapter.

Use the notebook you left on the TV to write down the names of the producers, directors, and _**casting directors**_ of the TV shows that you watch, as well as any movies you may rent or watch on cable. Take notes on the cast and characters, along with the story line. Story line is very helpful, because it can assist you in seeing how you would fit into a particular show. **A great site for episodic television research is www.epguides.com.**

No Credit at All . . .

Unfortunately, at the end of TV commercials, they don't say "Casting by___." This makes researching commercial casting directors a little more difficult, but not impossible. As you're watching TV, take note of the TV commercials that you like and that typically use talent of your type. Write down the name of the products—for example, Skippy Peanut Butter. Find a jar and look on the label for the name of the parent company. In this case, it's Unilever Bestfoods. Next, call their corporate office (most corporations have 800 numbers; often the number is on the label as well). Ask for their advertising department, and ask them which production company did their Skippy Peanut Butter spots, " . . . and while I have you on the phone, what other products does that production company handle for your company?" Now, call that production company and ask for the name of the casting director that did their Skippy Peanut Butter commercial, as well as any other commercials they may have cast recently. Keep all of this information in your notebook.

You can also log onto www.ecreativesearch.com, to track specific commercials and locate the casting directors. Now, as I said, researching information on a commercial casting director takes more time. But, that casting director will be impressed when they receive your cover letter!

BROADWAY—'The Great White Way'

Theater casting directors can also be researched. **Great sources of information on theater casting directors are www.playbill.com and www.theatredb.com**. Knowing which theater productions a casting director has cast will help you personalize your cover letters. You'll be able to add comments about the shows you have seen and the reviews you have read.

I have compiled a list of resource material that will help you find contact information for casting directors. You'll find the list of suggested resources in the back of this book. You can also obtain a list of casting directors and their show assignments from your local SAG office. For AEA show assignments, check the New York AEA Callboard daily for auditions or call the Los Angeles AEA office for casting listings.

EXERCISE #5
Using the worksheets in the back of the book, list five theatrical casting directors, five commercial casting directors, and three background casting agencies and/or services that you wish to target.

SCENE NINE
MARKET RESEARCH:
Organization and Application

YOUR DATABASE

Your *database* will consist of all the information you gather and organize. Whether you use a computer, binder, or a rolodex, neatly organize all of the contact information and notes from your worksheets and notebooks. This will be your database. From this, you will continue to build. Every time you meet someone in the entertainment industry, ask for business cards or contact information. This means everyone. Get phone numbers, addresses, and e-mails of other actors, acting coaches, casting directors, agents, managers, directors, producers, etc., and keep careful notes. Keep track of whom you meet, where and when you met, and what you talked about. All of this information will be crucial when you follow-up.

RESEARCH

You have identified the agents, managers, and casting directors you wish to target. You have compiled their contact information in what is now your database. These are the individuals to whom you will be writing in your initial mailing of *phase one* in your *marketing plan*. You will need to know something about them. This requires research. All of the information you gather will be added to your database.

"The Four Sensitive Areas"

Find out as much information as you can about the people to whom you will be writing. I suggest you learn what I call *"The Four Sensitive Areas": hometown, alma mater, children, and pets*. This information is not only useful when writing letters, but will certainly give you an edge when you get a meeting or audition. These are topics that encourage conversation, and will enable you to stand out and be remembered.

Professor Who?

No matter where we live, we never forget our hometown. When an actor walks into my office from Detroit, it's an invitation for a lengthy conversation. We all have memories of our hometown. No matter how long it's been since we graduated from high school or college, we never forget our alma maters. I find it so much fun to run into fellow alumni. I always ask questions like, 'Is Professor Stanton still teaching?' Like they wouldn't know how old I really am!

Marmalade?

Have you ever asked a parent if they had children, and when they answered "Yes," they didn't go on to elaborate? Have you ever asked a pet owner, "Do you have pets?" and they answer, "Yes," and that's it? I don't think so. I've never met a pet owner who didn't want to expound on the virtues of his dog, Rover, or orange cat, Marmalade; nor, have I ever met a parent that didn't feel compelled to elaborate on the talents and accomplishments of their sons or daughters.

TWO POODLES . . . and a son

Within the first five minutes of meeting me, there isn't anyone that doesn't know that I have a wonderful son and two spoiled Standard Poodles. No matter where I am or what I'm doing, I've always got time to talk about them. By researching agents, managers, and casting directors hometowns, alma maters, or whether or not they have children or pets, you open a door for conversation and great cover letters.

Gathering Information

Where do you find this information? Be creative. Periodicals such as *Backstage*, *Backstage West*, *Hollywood Reporter*, *Variety*, *In-Style Magazine*, *Entertainment Weekly*, and *Premiere* are a good starting point. Ask other actors about their agents and managers. Many agents, managers, and casting directors speak at cold read workshops. Find out where and when, and ask them questions yourself. They should feel flattered that you are so interested in where they got started, how they got started, and whether or not they have children or pets.

TRADE PUBLICATIONS

Trade publications and directories, are treasure troves of information. *Backstage West* (L.A. market), and *Backstage* (N.Y. market), for example, interview a casting director, producer, manager, agent or director in every issue. These publications list auditions for non-union and union theater, as well as union and non-union TV and film castings. Most importantly, for those new to the business or light on credits, they list auditions for student films and shorts.

"Who's on First?"

The *Hollywood Reporter* and *Variety* provide a great deal of valuable information. These publications follow the *'who's who'* in the entertainment business. Through them, you'll learn who's been hired or fired, who's been promoted or demoted, and who's moving to another agency, network, or studio. You will also learn about projects currently in development, pre-production, and production, as well as casting director assignments. It is vitally important for you to keep current on your industry. All businesses need to know and understand their markets.

Directories give names and addresses of every agent, casting director, manager, director and producer. There's a directory for everything. Read the trades and scour the directories. Transfer any and all pertinent information you find into your database. Your database will soon begin to grow and grow. You will find a list of recommended trades and directories in the back of this book.

ASSEMBLING A VIDEO LIBRARY

You should also assemble and maintain a video file, or *video library*, of the various prime time and daytime TV shows, as well as cable series shows like *Six Feet Under* and *The Shield*. When you have auditions for shows in production, you will be able to reference your tapes, and familiarize yourself with the type and style of the show. Is the show *naturalistic* or *broad comedy*? *Will and Grace* is broad, while *The Gilmore Girls* is more naturalistic. What is the show's genre? Is it sci-fi; action; or does it take place in a certain time period? What is the pace of the show? What types of characters are on the show, and how are they related?

As you assemble your library, keep track of the cast, directors, producers, and casting directors. Track down the names of the agents and managers of cast members on the shows for which you feel you are suitable. Keep all of this information in your database.

Purchase the industry directories, resource materials, and the various trade publications needed for your research. Be diligent with your notes, research, assignments, and exercises. Organize your data and information, and maintain a current video library. The time you invest in your career now will most certainly pay off for you in the future.

COVER LETTERS

You have identified the agents, managers, and casting directors you wish to target. You have your pictures and resumes. All you need now are 8x10 envelopes and stamps to begin your mailing, right? Wrong, you need a *cover letter*. You need a cover letter that is **personalized** and **professional**. Remember, this letter is your first impression. A personalized cover letter has a better chance of being read than one beginning, "Dear Casting Director" or "Dear _____," with the blank filled in. What do you do with mail that comes to you addressed 'Dear Occupant', or 'Resident?' Doing a mailing without a personalized cover letter is like throwing your picture and resume in the air and saying, "Whoever finds this, I love you!"

"Actors should always date their material; ALWAYS know the correct spelling of the person's name you are writing to; NEVER write 'To Whom It May Concern,' and GOD FORBID, NEVER address a cover letter to 'Dear Sirs,' because not everyone in this business is a 'sir.' Also, keep your letter to one paragraph; nobody has time to read anything more, if they even take the time to read the paragraph. (Lastly, and I know this is painstaking, pick out a famous person that you can compare yourself to, in order to make it easier for the agent/manager to 'place' you.)"
Melisa Birnstein, manager
Associated Artists Management, L.A.
www.associatedartistsmngt.com

Hopefully, you have done your homework. All of the questions you have asked, all of the research you have done, and the detailed notes you have taken will now help you to personalize and tailor each cover letter to the recipient of your pictures and resumes. Refer to your notes and research on the agents, managers, and casting directors you wish to target. When constructing a cover letter, the first paragraph should be about the person to whom you are writing, and why you are writing specifically to him or her.

Remember when you went to the theater, and asked that impressive actor about his manager?

Dear (Manager),

I went to a performance of *MM at 58: The Twilight Years* at the Zephyr Theater last night. I really enjoyed your client, Jane Doe. I think it's great you encourage your actors to do theater. I respect your good taste in clients, and would love to discuss representation with you. When can we meet?

In your letter, of course, you're going to mention how their client raved about them and that's why you're interested in a meeting.

Remember the notes you took while watching TV? All of the research you did to track down certain actor's agents will now be helpful.

Dear (Agent),

I was watching an episode of *Law & Order* last week and noticed your client, John Doe, had a small role in the courtroom scene. I know that it takes a hard-working agent to get a client on a top show. I'm looking for a hard-working agent to work with me. I know ten percent of nothing is nothing; however, I believe we can make money together. When can we meet?

Remember the notes you took watching movies?

Dear (Casting Director),

I rented *Titanic* again last week. It seems that I just can't see it enough. I thought the casting was right on. The supporting cast was so believable. I really cared about them. Billy Zane was a great choice. However, I was sorry he didn't go down with the ship. I'd love an opportunity to come in and read for you.

It's important for the person to whom you are writing knows they're important to you, and that you took time to find out something about them (without sounding like a stalker). Again, the first paragraph of your cover letter should be about them, the industry professional. The second paragraph should be about you. Your writing should show some personality. Show them an essence of you.

Remember that manager's interview that you read in Backstage*?*

Dear (Manager),

I enjoyed your interview in *Backstage*. I appreciated your honesty and your willingness to share. I was raised in Arizona as well, so I understand the climate both professionally and temperature wise. We should meet. I think that I have a lot to offer, and we seem to have similar experiences and goals. We both want to make money. I look forward to meeting with you at your earliest convenience.

Remember the cold read workshop you attended on agent's night, and asked all the right questions?

Dear (Agent),

I absorbed a great deal of information from your cold read workshop at the Casting Network. Your input was extremely beneficial. It was fun learning something about you. I too have two large standard poodles that I rescued. I agree, rescues are eternally grateful and loyal. If you're looking for a funny off-center dog lover, think of me.

ME. ME. ME.

Once you've grabbed the attention of the person to whom you are writing, tell them something about yourself. Most importantly, they need to know why they must meet you. Be positive. You wouldn't say, "I've only been in one film." You would say, "I've just completed my first film, and what an exciting experience it was. I learned so much."

> *"Actor's cover letters should be business like, but show personality; no name comparing, especially if I handle the actor. . . . such as 'I'm the next James Dean,' or 'I'm better than Chris Walken,' etc."*
> **Bill Treusch, manager**
> **Bill Treusch Associates, N.Y.**

Talk about your training and with whom you are training. Discuss any showcases or theater productions you are either currently or have been involved with in the past. If you're writing to a casting director, rave about your new or current representation. Name drop. If that casting director knows or respects your agent or manager, that may be reason enough for them to call you in.

It is also good to mention any callbacks you have had recently. Mention the names of the casting directors. If they are casting directors that other casting directors respect, you will have a better chance of being called in. The mere fact you were called back says a lot about your skills as an actor. For agents and managers, your next callback may mean money in their pocket!

The following is an edited excerpt from a letter a former student wrote:

I understand you are now part of the Party of Five *casting team. It's one of my favorite shows. The excitement starts building around 8:55 on Wednesday night in my house.* Party of Five *and popcorn . . . it's a ritual. Congratulations on such a successful show.*

I am a recent graduate of the University of California, Irvine. My training includes film/TV acting, improvisation, and musical theatre. I have just relocated to Los Angeles to put all of my training to use.

I would love the opportunity to meet with you so we can each put a face with the name. Please contact me at your earliest convenience. Thank you for your time and consideration.

Sincerely,
Aaron M. Revoir

ASSIGNMENT #3

Using the sample letters on the previous pages, write your own personalized cover letters. Write five letters to the theatrical agents and five letters to the commercial agents you wish to target.

Next, write five letters to the managers you wish to target.

Now write five letters to the commercial casting directors and five letters to the theatrical casting directors you will target.

ACT IV

MARKET AWARENESS AND DEMAND

"Always remember, 10 percent of nothing is nothing."
-Clair

SCENE TEN
PRODUCT EXPOSURE

MARKETING AND 'CREATING A NEED'

Shows like *Star Search*, *The Gong Show*, and *American Idol* have had success stories. However, the odds are not in the contestant's favor. Thousands upon thousands of people throughout the country brave the elements and spend hours in long lines for that one shot at stardom. These shows are for entertainment, and you are better off not considering them viable career launching platforms. The reality is, many viewers tune in to see the suffering and the humiliation of the losers, rather than to share in the glory of the winners. When it comes to your career, stick to a sound and professional marketing plan.

You have invested countless hours creating your database. You continually train and polish your skills as an actor. You have the perfect pictures and a professional looking resume. You have composed personalized and professional cover letters for each of your targeted agents, managers, and casting directors. Now comes the hard part, creating exposure and *creating a need* for your product. To do this, you must put together your *promotional plan*, and spend the rest of your career implementing it.

> *"The job of an actor is to be a self marketer."*
> **Brien Scott, casting director**
> **L.A.**

Perception Is Everything

Marketing is all about the consumer's perception of your business and the products you produce. The goal of any sound *marketing plan* is to entice the consumer to not only purchase your product, but to repurchase time and time again. To accomplish this, there must first be a need, either real or fabricated, for your product in the eyes of the consumer.

> *"In my estimation, marketing is most important in any actor's career. He/she has to get out (and) expose themselves to the Hollywood acting community. They should be in classes, appear in showcases, and do theater when (and) where possible."*
> **Barry Freed, agent**
> **Barry Freed Company, L.A.**

Creating or defining a need for your product is the first step when it comes to marketing your product. This need will induce consumers to try your product, but that's not good enough. For a business to survive, consumers must purchase, repurchase, and continue to repurchase your product. Offering quality and dependable products with competitive pricing is the only way to accomplish this. Continually training and striving to be the best at what you do, as well as maintaining a professional approach to your acting career, will help you and your business accomplish this. Your *promotional plan* will be the way in which you introduce, expose, and create the initial need for your product in the eyes of the consumers, the industry, and the market as a whole.

YOUR PROMOTIONAL PLAN

A sound promotional plan will generate exposure. 'Maximizing your exposure' is getting the 'biggest bang for your buck.' Actors generally have limited resources, minimal access to cash and credit, and very little time to waste. Hence the need for you to design a comprehensive, step by step plan to accomplish specific goals within your budget.

Distributor Interest . . .

Exposure creates interest and excitement. It is necessary to first generate interest from agents and managers, the distributors of your product. These are the people who will be selling you, and they must be excited about their product. Agents and managers have limited time and resources, as well. There is only enough time in a day to sell a certain number of products— or 'actors.' Therefore, they are going to devote their time selling the talents of those that have, or will have, the **highest** earning potential.

> *"Looking for an agent is not easy, but it can be done. Do what you can to get seen and get work. Sometimes the right agent will end up in the audience of a play you are in because a client of theirs is in the cast with you. A casting director might fall in love with you and connect you with their favorite agents."*
> **Josh Schiowitz, agent**
> **Schiowitz, Clay, Ankrum & Ross, Inc., L.A.**

"Which Client Are You?"

The typical working actor earns $678 a day, which is the scale rate for a SAG Day Player as of July 2003. Ten percent of that is approximately sixty-eight dollars. An agent has to devote a great deal of time and agency resources to book that job for you. Sixty-eight dollars is hardly motivation. Agents and managers must believe that your earning potential will grow in a relatively short period of time. As my son says, "There are clients who pay for their agent's BMW, and there are those who pay for the gas. Which client are you?"

"It's really all about the money. This is a business, and the numbers that a client makes is very important to me. I am a business and my work is for a fee. I only get paid when my clients work, so I'm in business to sign talent that will make me money, and that is not from an extra job or a one time co-star job. I need to have clients that will hit with a good booking within the first six months, and that is very realistic if there is talent."
Todd J. Stein, manager
Stein Entertainment Group, L.A.

Contact your local SAG office, or log onto www.sag.org for current contract rates.

Buyer Interest . . .

Next, you must generate interest and excitement in the people that will hire you, the buyers. The buyers are the casting directors, directors, and producers. They also have limited time and resources. What's going to make them want to spend the little time they do have in an overcrowded showcase theater with no air-conditioning? There are thousands of actors competing for a handful of jobs. Why should they take the time to meet with and/or audition you? The goal of your promotional plan is to answer these questions.

Starting with the Basics . . .

For the professional actor, there are many ways of creating exposure, and there are probably several that haven't been thought of yet. Start with the basics, and then get creative. Exposure can be gained through mailings, generals (interviews), showcases, theater, the use of promotional products or 'gimmicks,' and even working as an extra. Networking, joining professional organizations, and doing low budget—or as my son calls them, "no-budget"— films, as well as student films and shorts are also excellent ways to gain exposure.

There are directories and publications for actors, as well as web sites and internet services that are gaining popularity. Refer to the back of the book for resource listings.

"Marketing is very important for an actor. There are too many actors out there and too much competition, so anything you can do (short of being cheesy) to be noticed is a good thing. Postcards when you've got a nice role in a movie, TV show, or play are always a good idea. Make use of all your contacts, everyone else does."
Ginger Lawrence, agent
A House of Representatives, L.A.

MAILINGS

Mailings can be used to *introduce*, *keep in touch*, and to *follow-up*. Mailings come in many forms. They can consist of headshots and resumes, postcards, and industry comps (complimentary invitations) to a theater production or an industry showcase.

Mailings as an introduction are typically formal and are very effective. They consist of an 8x10 headshot, resume, and cover letter. The cover letters you have prepared are letters of introduction. Start at the top. You have targeted your first five choices for agents, managers, and casting directors. Now work your way down. You have to work, and to do this, you need an agent.

"As a personal manager, I know my needs. When I look at a picture and resume, I will know immediately if you might possibly fulfill those needs. However, like with all situations, time changes many things. I may lose a client down the road when he/she decides to change direction in careers. If I am not responding to your submission now, wait six months and try again."
Martin Weiss, manager
ETS Management, L.A.

NO Solicitors!

Unfortunately, any agent is better than no agent at all. Most production companies, studios, and networks will not accept unsolicited submissions. They solicit agencies for submissions, not the general public. Just having an agency name and logo on your picture is a plus. Pictures without representation, if they are not immediately discarded, will usually be considered last. Don't be discouraged if you are not represented. Do your mailings because you **can** be called in as an *independent* (unrepresented actor). It's just much easier to get meetings with an agent's or manager's logo.

"I open everything that arrives at my office. I keep what I feel is relevant to what I'm doing. . . . I keep those pictures (of actors) I find interesting and want to meet."
James F. Tarzia, CCDA, casting director
James Tarzia Casting, L.A.

"If we kept everything sent to us, the fire department would be at our door each day. I keep the pictures of people that I give callbacks and also that book the job."
Judy Belshe, casting director
Judy Belshe Casting, L.A.

Mailings to keep in touch can also be extremely effective. These mailings are typically less formal. Every time you get new pictures, change representation, or add new credits to your resume, send them out with a note. Let people know you're sending new pictures to update their files, and take the opportunity to let them know what you're up to. This is exposure.

Unfortunately, many envelopes containing pictures never get opened. And even if they do, they may not make it outside the mailroom or past an assistant. Many times, postcards can be more effective. Postcards don't need to be opened to know who sent them. Your picture and note are hard to miss. Postcards don't clutter desks like pictures do, and will often have a better chance of making it to the right people.

Postcards, however, should not be used as an introduction. The people to whom you send postcards to should already be familiar with you or your work through auditions, generals, showcases, CD workshops, or mailings. Otherwise, you're simply sending a small picture with no resume.

Drop Me a Line

There are many reasons to send a postcard with a note. Utilize postcards to let people know that you're performing in a theater production or showcase. Use postcards to inform people that you have a supporting role in a particular sit-com that airs Tuesday at 8 p.m. Let them know you have changed representation, you now have a manager, or you have been cast in a film. Again, *exposure!*

NEW REPRESENTATION!

ROBIN SYDNEY

Is

Now Represented

Theatrically and Commercially

by

XYZ AGENCY
(XXX) XXX-XXXX

"Only mail when you have something current going on, if you've been booked or if you have a new picture. If you know that you've sent me a picture in the past six months, I don't need another one. The best tool is a postcard. You can put on there what you are currently doing. This way you are keeping me updated as to the progress of your career and I'll see what type of roles you are being cast in."
Judy Belshe, casting director
Judy Belshe Casting, L.A.

"I like postcards when there is something to announce, like an agent change or a theater, film, or TV role. I particularly hate the Christmas cards with a photo stuck inside."
Rosemary Welden, CSA, casting director
L.A.

Be My Guest
 Postcards are great for inviting industry professionals to showcases and theater productions—complimentary, of course. Invitations have the best chance of making it past an assis-

tant. They are time dated, and not the type of thing you file. Most industry professionals utilize these occasions to find new talent, and will welcome the invitation. Once again, ***expo-sure***.

Don't Miss

Aaron Revoir

In

"XYZ THEATER PRODUCTION"

June 1st – 14th
at
THE ABC THEATER

Industry Comps Available
Reservations: (XXX) XXX-XXXX

Aaron Revoir

> " . . . send a postcard and follow up with a call. If you get a good
> vibe, maybe be a bit more persistent."
> **Vaughn D. Hart, agent**
> **Vaughn D. Hart & Associates, L.A.**

Mailings to follow-up are both effective and essential. These types of mailings are typically less formal, as well. Follow-up with an agent after a meeting. Thank them for their time. Follow-up with a casting director after an audition. Thank them for the opportunity. Follow-up with an industry professional that spoke at a showcase, class, or seminar. Thank them for their insight, and ask for a meeting.

> "If they (actors) are sending me a picture and resume, they should
> continually follow up with a postcard . . . an actor should send an
> 8x10 out to a casting director quarterly. In between those four
> months they should be in class and send postcards stating what they

are doing. No phone calls please. Casting directors need their privacy as much as actors do. Actors should never call a casting director unless the casting director called them or they were instructed to do so by their agent. Being an actor is not just having an agent or manager, it is promoting yourself."
Brien Scott, casting director
L.A.

Don't I Know You?

Do mailings frequently—at least every other month—to your designated targets. Although, you could also submit by e-mail, I would do both. This strategy takes time. The more mailings you do, the more familiar your name and face become. People may be convinced they know you. I've brought several actors in to read thinking I was familiar with them, only to find out we've never met. I've just seen their picture and followed their career via U.S. Mail.

"The Midas Touch"

Think about the way big companies advertise and market their products. I've never been in the market for a muffler, thankfully. But, if I ever do need a muffler, I'm going to Midas. Year after year, as long as I can remember, Midas has been reminding me they sell mufflers. For all I know, they invented them. Market yourself the same way.

"I do mailings personally every month, just to keep in the minds of the buyer. I feel the same for actors . . . an actor's picture and resume is their calling card and (they) should never stop sending them."
James F. Tarzia, CCDA, casting director
James Tarzia Casting, L.A.

As a casting director, up to now, I've never needed a 'YOU.' I didn't know 'YOU' existed. I've certainly managed this long without a 'YOU,' and I may never need a 'YOU.' But, if I do have a need for a 'YOU,' **I better know where to find you**. Let the industry know that this 'YOU' is available, how it works, and where we can see a test run. Show us why we need your product and where to find it in a hurry. Create the need.

Rare or Well-Done?

My son is a producer, and gets his fair share of mail. A fellow producer happened to be in his office when the mail arrived. This producer was talking about a cookware commercial his company was producing when he noticed a particular postcard in my son's stack of mail. The actor happened to be wearing a chef's hat, and coincidentally, was a chef. You guessed it . . . he got the job.

Regular or Premium?

Timing is everything. To the professional actor, exposure is everything. That particular actor did his mailings, did them well, and did them frequently. If he had gone to the beach instead of creating exposure through mailings, he would not have gotten cast. Only **you** can decide if you're going to be the actor who pays for his agent's BMW, or pays for the gas.

If you have representation, discuss the types of mailings and those you wish to target, with your agent and/or manager.

CD AND AGENT SHOWCASES

Casting director and agent cold read showcases are usually 'one-niters,' for which the actor pays a fee of about twenty to fifty dollars for a two to three hour period to meet and work with a member of the industry. This fee goes toward the showcase's overhead, mailings, advertising, and support staff. In addition, the casting director, manager, or agent is usually paid an honorarium to attend. I would suggest that your cold read skills be up to par prior to attending one of these showcases. Don't start doing the 'showcase circuit' until you acquire good cold read skills. As we have discussed, take a cold read audition class or workshop first.

Many of these workshops are known for the quality of their actors, and will often audition you before you take the workshop. This is a good thing. Honorarium or not, no respectable industry pro wants to waste his time.

Most workshops provide a monthly calendar of workshop guests. Check their calendars against the CD directories and TV show assignments to make sure they are listed as a casting director or an associate. If they're not listed, you may be paying to see an assistant without any decision-making power. If that's the case, save your money. There are too many viable casting directors to meet.

Here's the Catch . . .

You should also find out what the casting director is working on **now**—not what's in development, but what's on their desk currently. Here's the Catch 22 of CD showcases. If a casting director is currently casting a project or a show (which is what you want), they are often too busy to attend showcases. If they are between jobs, unemployed, and have the time, they are not in a position to cast you now.

Unless casting directors are attached to network shows, they attend workshops and showcases on their own time. The question is whether or not you should spend the money and risk they'll be working the week after you see them? Odds are, they will be working, probably sooner than later, and you won't be wasting your money. However, you should prioritize. First, see the casting directors that have show assignments or are currently casting, especially if you are on a tight budget.

A Little Controversy . . .

Presently, there is a controversy surrounding these cold read workshops and showcases. I approve of them. I have cast many actors from these showcases. Recently, I cast a film, and three of the four leading men were actors I found in various CD workshops. I think they are a great way for actors to meet and be seen. The down side is actors have to pay for a chance to meet and read for a casting director. The up side for many actors, especially those just starting out, is these workshops are their only chance to meet and read for a casting director. Whether you pay or not, it is exposure.

"Cold-reading workshops represent only one way for an actor to advance his/her career. Any actor who relies solely upon this method to get work is cheating himself. Workshops, however, are an excellent way practice audition skills and to network with industry professionals who daily see the triumphs and foibles of the auditioning actor. And equally important is the opportunity to forge strong relationships with casting directors; a networking possibility afforded many others job applicants in thousands of industries worldwide.

ITA is a place that is attended, managed and run by actors. Our primary purpose is to increase our acting and auditioning knowledge, learn the ins and outs of the audition process, and network in meaningful ways that benefit our careers. Anyone, either actor or casting director, who relies solely upon workshops as a means of meeting each other, is simply misusing the process. Workshops are only one way to learn and network. Cold reading workshops came under fire in 2001 when a few concerned citizens complained to the State of California that the workshops did not provide any benefit to actors, gave false hope to actors, and simply took actors money. Additionally, they claimed that casting directors had a conflict of interest since they are the ones who bring actors into the process of getting hired.

ITA, and the five other LAAWC members, are legally operating businesses. In our view, the process we underwent was necessary to prevent nefarious workshops from preying on actors and to ensure that the value of what we offer is verifiable."
Jean St. James
ITA Productions (CD Showcase)
www.itaproductions.com

I have recommended a few workshops on both coasts with which I am personally familiar. You will find them listed in the back of the book. Just make sure the person you are paying to see and audition for is in a decision-making position. In other words, can they make the decision alone to call you in for an audition? If it's an agent or an associate, do your homework. Make sure the person you are paying to see is not someone's assistant, or someone that works in the mailroom. This kind of exposure is costly, so spend your money wisely. If you're seeking representation, attending the 'agent nights' can be very beneficial.

INDUSTRY SHOWCASES

Prepared-scene industry showcases are usually about an hour in length. They consist of approximately twelve three-minute prepared scenes. This gives the industry an opportunity to meet and see the work of up to twenty-four actors in one night. These showcases can cost up to five hundred dollars per actor for two or three performances. This fee covers rehearsal time, direction, promotional materials, invitations, theater, food and follow-up. There are several reliable showcase producers, as well as schools and/or workshops that put on showcases that are well attended. Again, rely on word of mouth and reputation.

"I attend showcases and theater performances as often as my schedule permits, otherwise my associates attend. I attend all the university showcases. My associates attend showcases and theater twice a week. There are twelve Off Off-Broadway theaters where actors do showcases or produce their own shows to be seen."
Bill Treusch, manager
Bill Treusch Associates, N.Y.

More Homework?

Yes, more homework. Do your research. Ask casting directors, managers, acting teachers, and agents for referrals. Ask fellow actors to recommend industry showcases that have had good attendance. Stop by the theaters that provide space for industry showcases. Ask them to recommend a showcase for you. Join a good scene study group that will provide a showcase. Often, the coach or director will produce a showcase to 'showcase' their own teaching, or actors from a scene study group will produce a showcase themselves.

These industry showcases are, usually, well attended because they include a dinner or lunch buffet, the opportunity to schmooze with industry friends, and most importantly, to see new actors. Many showcases will also have an open bar, which may or may not be a good thing.

*"I do attend quite a few showcases, especially graduation classes of colleges and advanced acting classes. I advise actors doing showcases to do their homework, check out the reputation of the showcase, and find out if industry people do in fact attend. For new talent, this can be a good way to get noticed, but make sure you **1.** Do it for the right reasons. **2.** Have realistic expectations . . . a showcase is no guarantee of work. **3.** Prepare material that is actor appropriate and avoid scenes that are done to death; you don't want to be doing a scene (no matter how well written it is), for which another actor won a major award. All anyone will be thinking about is the other actor's performance and making comparisons to yours."*
Linda Phillips-Palo, CSA, casting director
Phillips/McGee Casting, L.A.

Union Support

SAG and *AFTRA* offer their members 'prepared scene nights' each month. Several industry guests are invited to observe the members' prepared scenes. There is no cost to members. The industry professionals donate their time in an effort to 'give back' to the acting community. SAG also offers its members a conservatory program, which includes seminars, workshops, film screenings, and an opportunity to be cast in AFI (American Film Institute) student films.

You will find a list of N.Y. and L.A. showcases in the back of the book.

EQUITY WAIVER THEATER AND INDUSTRY COMPS

As you are beginning to see, there are numerous ways for actors to create exposure. Proper exposure requires you 'to be seen.' The buyers need to know you exist. Equity Waiver (AEA's '99 Seat Plan') and showcase theater are great ways to gain exposure. I would equate this type of exposure to 'test-marketing' in the business world. Many companies test-market their products to get consumer input. That's what actors do by performing in Equity Waiver and showcase theater; they perform, they test-market themselves—not just to be seen, but to get a response from the industry, as well.

Equity (AEA) Waiver productions are held in theaters that have ninety-nine seats or less (AEA's '99 Seat Plan'). Equity Waiver enables union actors to grow artistically and be seen by 'waiving' union rules and contracts. *Backstage* and *Backstage West*, the *NY Times* and the *LA Times* review local, community, and Equity Waiver theater productions, as well as show-case productions that run a minimum of six weeks. If the theater's productions have been reviewed in the past, then it's a theater I would recommend. Be sure that the production has a publicist to handle press releases and over-see the promotion of the production.

> *"I prefer to think of it (Equity Waiver theater) as an opportunity. An opportunity to be seen, yes, but more; an opportunity to hone the valuable skills vital to the actor's growth and vital to the industry as a whole."*
> **Sonja Haney, casting director (Theater/AEA Waiver)**
> **The Strasberg Group, L.A.**

The main reason to give your time to showcase theater is to be seen. Before you audition, make sure the theater has safe, secure parking or valet service for industry guests and that they provide unlimited industry comps. Each industry guest will, usually, request two comps rather than go to the theater alone. If they don't provide you with industry comps, it can become rather costly, as you would have to pay for each ticket yourself. If you're going to do Equity Waiver theater, devote weeks of rehearsal time, and a minimum of six weeks of performance time while not being reimbursed financially, then you'll want to be sure that it's easy for the industry to come see you.

If you're seeking representation, "Keep yourself active in plays and invite agents. The actor should be aware that agents willing to see their work are spending their valuable time. Comps to agents are a must."
Laya Gelff, agent
Laya Gelff Agency, L.A.

Be sure you are cast in a role that will showcase your talents and type. This is not the time to stretch and challenge yourself; do that in scene study class. Perform the type of roles which you will likely be cast.

Curtain Going Up!

AEA theater auditions are held in L.A. for scheduled productions and tours. Contact your local AEA office for castings. In New York, check the AEA bulletin board for upcoming auditions. All castings are listed. AEA productions are a great way to earn a living and to be seen, especially if you're a 'triple threat' (an actor who sings and dances). AEA: **www.actorsequity.com.**

REGIONAL OPPORTUNITIES

Make a list of the cities where you have friends and/or family. These cities can provide you with outside-N.Y. or outside-L.A. opportunities for castings. Not only would you have a place to stay, with your training and marketing tools such as pictures, resumes, tapes etc., you would be more than competitive within those local markets.

Contact the local SAG or AFTRA offices in these cities for a list of agents. Contact the local film commissions for contact information on local SAG agents, managers, casting directors and production companies. Prepare a mailing to the local agents. Tell them you would like to have local representation and that you would be available on a *'local hire'* basis.

Local hire means you pay your own expenses and audition for the project locally. This saves the production company from paying for your travel, accommodations and per diem. You would be considered a *local hire*. This gives you an edge. You are L.A. or N.Y. trained, but they can cast you locally. The local agent gets the commission and you get the job. It's a win-win situation. This is also another way to work toward your SAG card. Local casting directors (cast local projects) or location casting directors (cast projects on location using local talent) can audition a non-union actor as a *local hire* far easier than auditioning a non-union actor in L.A. or N.Y. There are more Taft-Hartleys given on location than in L.A. or N.Y.

Arizona, for example, is a 'right to work' state and is in close proximity to Los Angeles. You can easily drive to Phoenix or Tucson for castings. Sign up with an Arizona agent and they'll call you for auditions, perhaps even get you in for callbacks so you don't have excessive travel. Many an actor has gotten a SAG card and built a tape by driving to states like Arizona. Washington, Oregon and Nevada are other possibilities close to Los Angeles. The more opportunities you explore, the sooner you will accomplish your goals.

Right to Work laws allow workers to decide whether or not they wish to join or financially support a particular union. Currently, there are twenty-two states with 'right to work' laws. For more information on 'right to work' laws: **www.fairmeasures.com.** For Arizona: **www.nrtw.org/c/azrtwlaw.htm.**

WORKING AS AN EXTRA

'Extras,' or *'Background Atmosphere,'* are essential in film and TV. They bring scenes to life. Imagine a scene on a bus without passengers, a mall without shoppers, or a New York street without pedestrians. It wouldn't be very realistic or believable. All of the people you see milling around behind the scenes are cast and paid. In fact, many of the extras you see are members of SAG.

Many extras are professional actors who are between jobs. There are professional extras, as well. Extra work is extremely flexible. An actor need only give his extra agency or agencies a day's notice regarding availability. Because of the flexibility, it can be a good way for an actor to earn money. There are differing opinions as to professional actors working as extras. Consult with your agent or manager before accepting extra work.

"I would recommend an actor work as an 'extra' on feature films only. If television casting directors see an actor doing TV extra work, they tend to assume that is all the actor is capable of doing."
Melisa Birnstein, manager
Associated Artists Management, L.A.
www.associatedartistsmngt.com

"An actor is a performer. An extra is a piece of cardboard. If a person wishes to learn what life is like on the set, then work one job as an extra and treat it like a paid-off parking ticket . . . put it in your past and forget it ever happened."
Martin Weiss, manager
ETS Management, L.A.

A Face in the Crowd

Production companies use extra casting agencies or services. In many instances these agencies will submit pictures based on the type of extras needed for the scene. A production may need students for a scene in a high school or soldiers for a battle scene. They may require anything from Wall Street executives to gang members. Each and every scene requires certain stereotyped looks, not just bodies. Age, gender, and ethnicity are often crucial requirements in extra casting.

Certain scenes may require extras to have particular skills such as skating, riding a bike, or surfing. Extras who are cast to perform these types of skills are given a 'bump' (increase) in pay. In many cases, they will bring their own bikes, or surfboards, for which they are paid even more.

Benefit with Benefits . . .

Many SAG members work as extras. They are paid a SAG 'extra rate,' and enjoy many of the benefits of those with lines. These benefits include meal penalties, overtime, and mileage. SAG also protects its members from unsafe and improper working conditions, as well as ensuring its members are paid properly and on time. Working as an SAG extra also helps qualify members for insurance benefits. To qualify for insurance, you must earn a certain amount of money each year working as a SAG member. Check with your local SAG office to get current qualifying rates and guidelines, as they vary.

Every SAG production is required to hire a certain number of SAG extras and SAG stand-ins before they are allowed to hire less expensive non-union extras. This number is based on the budget and length of production. SAG will usually insist that all stand-ins be SAG members, and require productions to hire about thirty SAG extras a day before they are allowed to hire less expensive non-union extras.

"Thank You"

Working as an extra is a good way to network with other actors, learn about film and TV production, and to gain exposure. Often times, at the last minute, extras will be given unscripted lines. The director may decide he wants the cashier in a scene to say, "Thank you," or a pedestrian to yell at a passing motorist. Boom! Just like that, you're a *Day Player*. If you are not a SAG member, the production must Taft-Hartley you, which as we discussed, means you are now SAG eligible.

Getting lines means you just got a big pay raise, not to mention *residuals*. Residuals are monies paid to all SAG actors over the life span of the film or TV show. Residuals are paid based upon video and DVD sales, as well as TV and cable airings. Every time the show airs, you get paid. For further information on residuals, check with your local SAG office.

You will find a list of extra casting agencies and/or services in the back of the book.

GENERALS

Generals, or *'general auditions,'* are interviews, first meetings, and you guessed it, *exposure*. Generals are an opportunity to say, "Hello!" Agents and managers make every attempt to get their clients out to meet with casting directors. A general is an introduction to a casting director. It's an opportunity to put your headshot and resume, along with your demo-tape, into their hands personally. It is an opportunity to impress them with your research—for example, "I heard you were from Detroit, my Father was raised in Detroit." This is a great opener. It gives you and the casting director a common ground, "I really enjoyed your last project; you must have had fun working on it." As you can see, your database will become more and more valuable. Once you've had a general with a casting director, it will be easier for your agent or manager to get you in for an audition, since they now know who you are. Generals are also the time for those great monologues you've been working on in class.

> *"The doors are more open in New York. Once a month AEA
> requires agents to have an open call for actors. Agents may
> hate this, but it's an AEA rule."*
> **Bill Treusch, manager**
> **Bill Treusch Associates, N.Y.**

PROMOTIONAL PRODUCTS, GIMMICKS AND GIFTS

Actors can be very clever and creative. Being creative is a good thing. However, there are lines that when crossed, will backfire. There is a difference between being creative and being silly.

Everyday, you see examples of the various types of promotional products companies use. Some companies will give their customers things like coffee mugs, pens, calendars, or refrigerator magnets branded with their company's logo. Others use shirts, hats, bumper stickers, etc. Many actors do similar things.

A Weekly Thought . . .

An actor once sent me a ruler with his name and phone number on one side, and written on the other side was *"just wanted to get my foot in the door."* That was years ago, but I still remember the actor who sent it. Another actor sent me a postcard with a "thought for the week" on it. The actor included his name, but no other information. It was cute, so I tacked it up on my bulletin board. I continued to receive postcards with great quotes, prose, poems, and humorous thoughts every week for a couple of months. Then one week, they stopped. The following week, the actor called. I asked him where my weekly thought was, and he replied, "I'll bring it over." I said "fine!" and he got his general.

"As a manager, I am involved with a client's marketing. We wrote a pitch letter to get one of my clients a theatrical agent. The letter opened with, 'My client, Jane Doe, would like to buy you a new Mercedes. Call at once to set up a meeting and discuss colors'."
Brian Funnagan, manager
Brian Funnagan Management, L.A.

Will She Ever Stop Talking About Her Dogs?

Knowing that I have two wonderful, but spoiled Standard Poodles, several actors have sent me dog toys and treats for my 'girls,' Poodle calendars, articles on Poodles, dog shows, and rescues. In fact, that's how I rescued my first Standard Poodle. We had just lost a white Standard Poodle that had been a part of our family for thirteen years, and an actor was kind enough to send me information about Standard Poodle rescues. I've rescued four great friends since then, and still have two.

"There is an actor who sent me a post card and on it he had printed copies of all the posters from all the movies I had done. Amazing. I didn't even know some of these movies had posters. But it showed me he had done his homework on who I was."
Linda Phillips-Palo, CSA, casting director
Phillips/McGee Casting, L.A.

I once mentioned at a CD workshop, that I loved ballet. From then on, a particular actress would send me notices when the ballet was in town. Since it's not often that I take the time to read newspapers other than the trades, I appreciated the info and was able to enjoy many performances thanks to her thoughtfulness. Of course, all these marketing examples were accompanied with a picture and resume.

"The absolute worst thing an actor did was walk down the hall to my office when I was casting a 'police/psycho killer movie' and stab a knife into my door. He walked out, but I was scared. I didn't know how real his motivation was or if he was just plain crazy."
Linda Phillips-Palo, CSA, casting director
Phillips/McGee Casting, L.A.

I've given you some examples of actors being creative. Try to be creative yourself.

Save the Cookies for Santa

'Thank You' cards are a polite and professional way to follow up, especially if you were just cast. Inexpensive gifts are only appropriate in certain situations. A gift and a 'Thank You' card would be appropriate for a casting director if you were cast. Never send gifts for representation or auditions. Avoid expensive gifts because they will make people uncomfortable, and it's not necessary. Don't send home cooked food—it will only be thrown out. Don't sneak onto studio lots or show up at someone's office unannounced or uninvited. And most importantly, **NEVER CALL OR SHOW UP AT SOMEONE'S HOME UNLESS YOU ARE INVITED TO DO SO**. They may think you are a stalker. Don't take chances with your reputation.

> *"If I cast someone in a movie, a gift is a very nice thank you . . . and who doesn't love flowers? But, if it is after an audition only, it seems inappropriate."*
> **Rosemary Welden, CSA, casting director**
> **L.A.**

> *"All the gimmicks in the world won't help if you can't deliver the goods."*
> **Linda Phillips-Palo, CSA, casting director**
> **Phillips/McGee Casting, L.A.**

THE PERSONAL WEB SITE

You can create your own web site or have one professionally created for you. Today, the vast majority of companies use web sites to market and sell their products. Your web site would show your product, your picture and resume, as well as your reel.

> *" . . . every time you can increase your marketing tools it helps, but agents don't always have time to go to the web site, so I don't think it's a necessity."*
> **Melisa Birnstein, manager**
> **Associated Artists Management, L.A.**
> **www.associatedartistsmngt.com**

Having your demo on a web site saves you the cost of getting videotapes or CDs out to the industry, and is a quick casting reference. In your cover letter you refer to your web site and suggest they log on to see your work. Although having your reel available on the Internet does not eliminate the need for a demo reel, it does give you one more tool to use when marketing your product, and it's more exposure.

"With the expansion of the Internet over the past decade, many people (including industry oriented professionals) search the web for many of their needs. A web site can act as a business card for actors, and these particular business cards have led to both auditions and fan recognition. Not only is a web site helpful in the 21st century, it's nearly becoming mandatory."
Martin Weiss, manager
ETS Management, L.A.

Because many industry people are not computer savvy, your web site should be easy to use. A web site is another liaison between you and the industry, so put thought into the design and obtain professional help.

THE ACADEMY PLAYERS DIRECTORY

The *Academy Players Directory* is a directory of professional actors. The directory will list your photo, union affiliations, and contacts. The *Academy Players Directory* is distributed to CSA (Casting Society of America) casting directors, and the majority of agents and managers use them for reference, as well. An agent can tell a casting director, "My client is on page 34, and his resume with a clip from his last film is on the Academy Players web site".

Placing your photo and resume in the *Academy Players Directory* for L.A., automatically puts you on their web site. You can also update your resume on their site. By listing in the *Academy Players Directory*, you are also on *The Link*, which is an Internet submission service for agents. The Academy of Motion Picture Arts and Sciences and Breakdown Services together created *The Link*.

For more information, log onto:
The Academy Players Directory: **www.acadpd.org**
The Players Guide in NY: **www.playersguideny.com**
Breakdown Services: **www.breakdownservies.com**

INTERNET SERVICES

Castnet is an Internet casting service that enables actors to post headshots and resumes online for a yearly fee. For additional fees, you can post clips from your demo reel. Actors can submit to agents online for representation and submit photos online to casting directors. Members feel they save on mailings, as well as the cost of photos and demos. Castnet is also used as a casting tool. Casting directors can search through the headshots and resumes that are posted. Again, services like this do not eliminate the need for mailings. These services should be considered supplemental marketing tools only. Consult with your agent or manager before subscribing to any internet casting services.

"Personally, I don't like them and don't use them. I like the personal touch. I want to talk to the actor's representative, get the pitch."
Breanna Benjamin, casting director
Breanna Benjamin Casting, N.Y.

"I think they are ridiculous—you have to meet people. Send a photo with a cover letter and set an appointment. How can you cast from the Internet? This is a people business."
Bill Treusch, manager
Bill Treusch Associates, N.Y.

"I think having actors' pictures and resumes available online is wonderful. Sometimes a role needs to be cast immediately, and it's much easier to go to online submissions than wait for pictures to be delivered."
Stanzi Stokes, CSA, casting director
Stanzi Stokes Casting, L.A.

Like Breakdown Services, Castnet gives actors the ability to download sides, as well as providing access to the breakdowns that are posted. Welcome to the 21st century. Showfax is a service that allows you to obtain sides for your auditions. For a small fee, actors have access to their sides 24/7. Breakdown Services: **www.breakdownservies.com,** Castnet: **www.castnet.com,** Showfax: **www.showfax.com.**

NETWORKING

Networking, I'm sure, began in Hollywood. There are many networking groups and professional organizations available to those in the entertainment industry. It's comforting to share your experiences and communicate with other industry professionals, especially for actors. Here are a few of the organizations with which I am familiar in L.A. There are many others worth checking out, so ask around.

Women in Film (WIF) is a great networking group for men and women. I've been a member of WIF for many years. There are monthly breakfast meetings throughout the city. You can go to the one near you or attend any and all of them. Each breakfast has an industry guest, and I myself, have been a guest speaker several times. The breakfasts are informative and fun. WIF annually presents the 'Crystal Awards,' and also offers industry-related workshops, seminars, and mixers. Women in Film: **www.wif.org.**

The American Film Institute encourages and develops new talent. An open membership offers workshops and seminars. AFI is well known for its two-year accredited program in directing, producing, writing, and production. AFI: **www.afionline.org.**

The Actors Network is a networking group for professional actors. Members have access to resources such as a library, discussion groups, and guest speakers. I've also been a guest for The Actors Network. The Actors Network: **www.actors.network.com.**

The Academy of Television Arts & Sciences (ATAS) award the *'Emmys'*, annually. They offer workshops and host luncheons and screenings. I've been on the faculty of their repertory group and participated as an actor, as well. A wonderful organization if you qualify. ATAS: **www.emmys.org.**

The Academy of Motion Picture Arts & Sciences (AMPAS) award the *'Oscars'* annually. If you qualify, this too, is a wonderful organization. AMPAS: **www.ampas.org.** or **www.oscars.org.**

The American Theatre Wing annually awards the Antoinette Perry *'Tony'* Award for theater excellence. If you qualify, this is another wonderful organization. The American Theatre Wing: **www.tonys.org.**

Independent Feature Producers West (IFP) presents the *'Spirit Awards'* annually. Again, if you qualify, this is a great networking group. **IFP West: www.ezentertainment.net/ indiespirit.htm.**

TALENT AND MODEL CONVENTIONS

Talent and model conventions are a great way to see and be seen by the industry. I attend the *International Modeling and Talent Association (IMTA)* conventions in Los Angeles each January and in New York each July. IMTA is an association of highly regarded training centers and talent and modeling agencies throughout the U.S., Canada, Mexico, Australia, South America, and Europe. The member training centers include both independent and franchised centers such as Barbizon. These conventions give aspiring actors, models, singers, and dancers the opportunity to perform in front of hundreds of modeling and talent agents, personal managers, and casting directors from every major market worldwide. I've seen young talent walk away with agent and manager offers, major auditions, and contracts with European modeling agencies. Well known actors like Elijah Wood, Ashton Kutcher, Jessica Biel, and Katie Holmes have participated in IMTA conventions. To locate a training center near you, contact IMTA. IMTA: **www.imta.com.**

"New artists are the lifeblood of the music business. Finding tomorrow's stars today is something I try to do on a daily basis. That task is made easier at the IMTA competitions. I regularly attend IMTA to scout for new talent. When I discover someone with 'star' potential, I usually invite them into my studio for an audition. If successful, I move forward with producing a demo package consisting of three or four strong songs which I then play for various recording companies. I love the creative freedom and the fresh approach that can be taken with new and developing artists."
Michael Jay, music producer
Jambo Productions, L.A.

Professional Model & Talent Training Centers showcase their graduates. Franchised schools such as Barbizon give their graduates an opportunity to perform on both the runway and on camera. Local and major-market industry professionals are invited to attend. These showcases are popular. After all, who doesn't want 'first look' at a new talent? For information: **www.barbizonmodeling.com.**

*"Industry leaders have asked me for years to showcase our
. . . Barbizon students and graduates. Last year, I did a Barbizon
showcase where industry leaders from fashion as well as talent
attended. Many new faces were discovered."*
Charles Nemes, president
Barbizon Royal, Chicago

PUBLIC ACCESS TELEVISION

All major cities have *public access* television stations. Working as a volunteer or intern at one of these stations is a great way to learn camera, directing, producing, etc. Public access programs need actors, as well. Drop a picture and resume off at the stations, introduce yourself, and let them know you are interested and available for upcoming projects. Better yet, come up with an idea for your own weekly show.

My friend, Judy Kerr, has a weekly acting workshop on a public access station. She interviews different industry guests and uses her students for acting exercises. Another actor I know produces a 'new age' talk show on a public access station. Coming up with your own show idea and being your own producer is another way to create exposure and gain experience. Contact your local public access stations for more information.

ACT V

PRODUCT SALES

"The time to be nervous is when you don't have an audition,
not when you do."

-Clair

SCENE ELEVEN
MEETINGS: 'THE PERSONALITY AUDITION'

SELLING YOURSELF

Know Yourself. Be Yourself. Sell Yourself. You must first learn to market and sell your-self as 'YOU,' before you can sell yourself as *'product.'*

The amount of time it takes to refine your product, prepare and execute a competent, thorough, and professional marketing plan, and create exposure through creative promo-tional plans and networking is immense. The hours upon hours of research, and the tedious process of creating a database, can be discouraging. Will it ever end?

The answer is simple, yes and no. Yes, it gets easier. No, the process of marketing, cre-ating exposure, and refining your product does not end.

As you embark on your career, you must distinguish between short and long-term goals. You also must make distinctions between goals and dreams. Being a *'star'* may be your dream, and dreams do come true. However, your ***long-term goal*** is to become a working actor. Your ***short-term goal***, the fruit of all your hard work, is to get that call, to get that ***meeting***.

MEETINGS

For the professional actor, a ***meeting*** is an ***interview***, and an interview is a *'personality audition.'* Meetings are introductions, your chance to introduce yourself to those in the industry who can help you. Meetings are just that, meetings, and are typically informal. Occasionally, you will be asked to cold read or do a prepared monologue. But, most of the time, the person or persons with whom you are meeting, just want to get to know you. Meetings are your opportunity to show some charm and personality. Hence the term, *'per-sonality audition.'*

"The things I look for in potential clients are personality and willingness of the parent to take their child on auditions. Young adults must have dedication, availability and talent."
Vivian Hollander, agent
Hollander Talent Group, Inc., L.A.

All of the hard work involved in marketing yourself, sending mailings, and creating exposure is for one thing, to get that meeting. Agents and managers will meet with you to discuss possible representation. Casting directors use meetings to keep up on the new and available talent pool. What type are you? How do you carry yourself? Do you present yourself confidently and professionally? Do you speak well, and clearly? What kind of background, training, and *personality* do you have? These are all things looked for in meetings.

> *"It's important for an actor to be on time, prepared, and look great. They may not book a particular job, but if they've left a positive impression on the casting director, they may be called in for future projects."*
> **Charity Marquis, agent**
> **Osbrink Models & Talent, L.A.**

PREPARING FOR MEETINGS

Be on time for your meeting. Never be late. In fact, it would be wise for you to start getting used to being early. Get any directions or reference any maps you might need to get to your meeting prior to embarking on your commute. Have money for parking. Know and commit to memory the name or names of the people with whom you are meeting. Show up well groomed and well rested. It is important to get plenty of sleep the night before a meeting. You want to be sharp, and you don't want to look tired. Dress appropriately for your age and wear comfortable clothes. This in not the time to wear something new—you don't want to be thinking about your wardrobe. Keep it simple. And lastly, you want to show up prepared.

> *"To misquote an old adage, 'Parents should be seen and not heard'. It is very important that your child be able to communicate with agents and casting directors one on one. Parents are never allowed into the casting session, so your child should feel comfortable talking with adults, and answering their questions. Your job as a parent is to be there for your child, encourage them, and give them lots of support."*
> **Jan Brown, manager**
> **JDS Management, L.A.**

"I interview the child by themselves with Nicole, my partner, then we bring the parents in and speak with them. If we have a red flag about the parent, it doesn't matter how great the kid is, we don't take them on."
Carolyn Thompson-Goldstein, agent
Amsel, Eisenstadt & Frazier, Inc., L.A.

Everything but the Kitchen Sink

When meeting with agents and managers, bring all of your marketing tools with you to the meetings. Bring your pictures and resumes. Bring all of your contact sheets and proofs because there may be other photos they prefer. Agents and managers do like to pick out the photos they will be submitting to sell you. If you have been doing any commercial or fashion print, bring your portfolio so they can see your tear sheets and test shots.

*"The number one piece of advice I can give young actors seeking representation is always be prepared and give more than what they ask for. Go into an audition ready to do a great monologue and a really energetic commercial. Have up-dated pictures and resumes, and don't forget to **bring them with you everywhere**.*
Keep your materials in your car ready to be given out. Think of them as your business cards. Don't get discouraged. If you are choosing this field to get into, then remember you will ALWAYS be interviewing! No matter what level you might get to, there will always be another person to make a good impression with."
Carolyn Thompson-Goldstein, agent
Amsel, Eisenstadt & Frazier, Inc., L.A.

If you will be interviewing for voice-over work, bring your voice demo, and leave it for them to listen to and critique. They may want to use it as is, re-cut it, or toss it out. They will let you know how many copies they need. Take all criticism in a positive way, and remember they are trying to help and know what they will need to sell you. If you have a demo tape, leave it with them to view and comment.

Just the Kitchen Sink

When meeting with casting directors, bring your pictures and resumes. If you have pictures that show different looks, bring them, too. Bring any demo reel you might have. And again, be prepared to leave it. Never give out your only copy. You probably won't get it back, so don't ask. Casting directors, or anyone else not directly associated with fashion or commercial print, will not be interested in your portfolio. Don't offer it. The same goes for voice and singing demos, unless it's a voice-over audition or you're auditioning for a role that requires singing.

Ask . . . Listen . . . Care . . .

During your interview, the casting director, agent, or manager may or may not interject comments or questions. If they do, that's the time to bring up, "We went to the same school together" or, "I read that you graduated from the University of Michigan." This is a good time to interject any information you've learned about the casting director, agent, or manager. Keep the conversation flowing. *Ask* questions about them. *Listen* to their responses. *Care* about who they are and what they say. Actors are not the only ones with egos.

Please . . . NO SHAKESPEARE!

It's a good idea to have several contemporary monologues ready to deliver. Make sure your *monologues* are suitable for your type and age, and can be delivered in a small office across from a desk. Don't costume or bring props. Your monologue should be delivered in such a natural way that no one should know you're delivering a monologue. It needs to be believable and suitable. You are in an office, not on stage, so conversational dialogue is a must. Keep movement to a minimum. Use the space you have and deliver as you would if you were simply talking, not performing someone else's words.

It's Cold . . .

You may also be asked to *cold read*. The majority of auditions are cold reads, so it's only natural that an agent or manager will want you to cold read in order to see how you will do in an audition situation. Their name will be on your pictures and resumes, and casting directors will often audition a new talent because of their relationship with the agent or manager. Good, solid cold read skills are a must. If you are asked, take a few minutes to look over the script. Sit in the reception room and do not disturb them. Only an amateur would try to cold read without studying the script.

Looking Good, Feeling Good

Wonderful first impressions begin with confidence. Don't confuse confidence with conceit. Conceit signals a lack of confidence. To be confident, you must feel good about yourself. Your insecurities are easy to pick up, even if you believe you hide them well.

"I not only look for a client who is unique, both in their talent and their look, but in their presence." I look at " . . . the way they handle themselves, their confidence, and bottom line, honesty in a performance. It has to be real."
Bruce Economou, manager
John Crosby Management, L.A.

Actors tend to be extremely insecure, and rightly so. Most actors are not hired or fired based upon merits, qualifications, or expertise. Most actors are cast based upon appearance and type. Don't get me wrong, your skills and talents are essential, but getting the audition will likely be based upon your looks.

Only you know what your insecurities are and only you can work on them and change them. You may not be overweight, but if you think you're overweight, it will show. It will show in the way you walk, talk and sit. If you think you're overweight, then consult with your doctor about dieting. Your doctor will probably prescribe a healthy diet and regular exercise. If you don't think your teeth are straight or white enough, consult with your dentist and fix them. If glasses make you feel uncomfortable, see your optometrist about contacts. Otherwise, get comfortable in your own skin, and like who you are.

*"**Having a sense of humor, in this town, about yourself and about Hollywood is an absolute necessity for one's mental health.** Never take anything personally; be prepared to have major ups and downs (being resilient is important); study, study, study; stay in a play, on a set, doing independent stuff, through backstage, etc.; always keep your word."*
Melisa Birnstein, manager
Associated Artists Management, L.A.
www.associatedartistsmngt.com

THE PERSONALITY AUDITION

A meeting or interview is what I call a *'personality audition.'* Your personality is what makes you unique and different from anyone else. From the moment you walk in the door, be yourself. This is not the time to put on an act. An actor's personality is what brings the roles or characters he plays to life. That's what casting directors, agents, and managers look for during meetings. When we watch our favorite actors in various films or TV shows, it's their own particular personalities and what they bring to their characters that we want to see.

Actors play different types of roles. Whether they are playing comedic or dark roles, good guys or bad guys, their personalities come through. That is what we like about their characters.

A meeting is not a popularity contest. They are not deciding whether or not they like you, so don't try to make them like you. Trying too hard will make you appear insecure and desperate. Liking you is a plus, but is not necessarily a determining factor. Agents and managers are trying to determine whether or not they can sell you. Can you make them money? Casting directors want to look good to the directors and producers for whom they work. Before an actor is cast, roles are just lifeless words on paper. Often, a director won't know what he is looking for until he finds it. If you are brought in to audition, will you make the casting director look good? Showing some personality and being yourself is the only way they will be able to determine that.

Vulnerability Sells

Vulnerability sells. The more you reveal of yourself, the more vulnerable you are. Just be honest about who you are, without any pretenses. We often try to hide or mask our feelings when we are nervous, uncomfortable, or insecure. Rather than trying to hide your feelings, accept them and go with them. Be yourself. Don't try to be anything you're not. That's why it's called a 'personality audition.' People want to know what you're going to bring to a role. If you were the character, how would you react? How would you respond?

PREPARING FOR THE PERSONALITY AUDITION

Understanding what the industry is looking for is important. It is also important to know what to expect, and what is expected from you during meetings. Having an idea of the types of questions you will be asked, and being prepared to answer them, will be crucial in your success. *The most difficult role you will ever play is yourself.*

"So, Tell Me About Yourself"

The dreaded question. Every casting director, manager, and agent will inevitably ask you to tell him or her *'about yourself.'* That's always hard to answer, especially when you're sitting in a room full of strangers. It is especially difficult when you're not prepared. Why is it so difficult? What subject does any of us know more about?

The problem is that so many of us have a chameleon-like attitude. We want to fit in, and we want to be liked. When asked to talk about ourselves, we are more concerned with giving the response we think people want to hear, rather than answering the question truthfully. It is also possible that we have answered these types of questions with some sort of upbeat, life is grand, politically correct spin so often, we've lost touch with who and what we really are.

If this sounds like you, it's time to change. The fact is, when you portray yourself as anyone or anything other than who you really are, the only one being fooled is YOU. We think the way we think. We feel the way we feel. And our opinions are just that, our opinions. There are no right or wrong answers; they're our opinions. What I'm saying is, you must be comfortable with and like yourself, before others will be comfortable with and like you. You may need to reacquaint yourself with you.

"What Have You Been Doing Lately?"

The second inevitable question is, "So what have you been doing lately?" This is your opportunity to let them know where you can be seen if you're in a play, a showcase, or appearing on a TV show next week. This is also the opportunity to let them know you're a working actor—maybe not an employed one but, certainly a working one. You're working on pictures, updating your resume, and attending classes and/or workshops.

Sometimes our eccentricities are really interesting; sometimes they are not. The following exercises will help you prepare for these types of questions, and more importantly, will help you get reacquainted with yourself.

Your 'Commercial'

Now you are ready to prepare a 'commercial' for your product. Your commercial should be a sixty-second 'spot,' selling you. Ford does it, and so can you.

You must be real and natural, not rehearsed. What your commercial will be is sixty-seconds worth of fun, informative, and interesting information about you: who you are, and what makes you 'tick.' Preparing a commercial for your product will help you become more familiar with 'YOU.'

Commercials

There are many types of commercials. Companies like *Pepsi*, are interested in name or brand recognition and holding or increasing their *market share*. Simply put, if you took the total number of carbonated soft drinks sold in a given period of time, the percentage of those soft drinks that were Pepsi products would be termed their market share. When choosing a cola, Pepsi wants you choosing a Pepsi. Their commercials tend to be exciting, funny, catchy, and memorable. They don't talk about ingredients or benefits.

Commercials for cars, health, and beauty products, or even your local exterminator, are much more informative. Usually in about thirty-seconds, they tell you the name of the product, what the product is, why you need it, what makes it unique, why it's better than other like products, where you can get it, and sometimes, what will happen if you don't buy their product. Termites will eat your house, women won't like you, or your dishes won't be squeaky clean.

Now it's time to prepare for your personality audition by preparing your ***commercial***. Being prepared will be helpful in meetings and interviews. The next time you're asked, "Tell me about yourself," you will have a starting point. When the auditor interjects comments or questions, maintain the conversation and then go back to your commercial. Keep in mind, truth in advertising is important. In other words, be honest, truthful, and **be yourself**.

EXERCISE #6

Get to know yourself. Using your notebook, write down the five most interesting things about you. What makes you different? What makes you unique? We're all unique, and we're all very special in our own ways. Take your time.

Remember, just because it happened to you, doesn't make it interesting.

"Five Things"

You know what your product is and does, and hopefully you know your name. The five interesting things about you will be the body, the informative part, of your ***commercial***. For example, you may raise Dalmatians or run marathons. Perhaps you play an instrument or were born in Tibet. What stands out? What makes you different? What do you do that nobody else does?

Stay away from all areas that could be awkward or uncomfortable for the other person. Avoid anything negative or embarrassing. For instance, if you or your parents are going through a divorce, keep it to yourself. What would you say if someone walked into a room and said, "Hi, I'm Joanne and my husband just left me?" There would be several uncomfortable seconds of silence, and then you would probably want to excuse yourself. Avoid those moments like the plague. Keep it 'up,' interesting, and positive.

My Way

Once you come up with the five most interesting things about you, come up with creative ways to express yourself and reveal the information. "My favorite flavor is vanilla," is neither interesting nor informative. Being from Tennessee, like my friend Jackie, is mildly interesting at best. It's the way she tells people that makes that information interesting. Jackie will say, "I'm from Tennessee. I don't have an accent, but I still go without shoes as much as possible." Statements like this are cute and invite a response, which will likely get you out of the 'hot-seat' and land you in a two or three-way conversation.

When asked what the five most interesting things were about them, some former students wrote the following:

- "I think of myself as a Southern Woman with a West-Coast heart. Think Scarlet O'Hara in a Yoga class!"
- "I'm just a country gal in stiletto heels, loving every moment of the pinched toes."
- "In high school, I was voted 'most thoughtful' and 'class flirt.' I guess that makes me a thoughtful flirt!"
- "I believe in making lemonade when life hands me lemons. I drink a lot of lemonade."
- "I stop to smell the roses. I stop to touch them as well. I go crazy when I touch them, I want to eat them!"
- "I like to get in my car and just drive until I run out of gas."

EXERCISE #7

Using your notebook, write down some creative ways to describe the 'five most interesting things about you'. How are you going to tell people, "This is who I am?" Again, have fun and take your time.

Remember, if you're not funny, don't try to be funny. Be yourself.

The 'Hook and Tag'

Every good commercial has a *'hook'* and a *'tag.'* The *hook*, or *'handle,'* gets people interested so they want to learn more. It's your opening line—something other than, "Hi!" or "How are you?" Your *hook* is a creative and interesting way to say, "This is who I am." The tag line is what leaves them remembering the product. In your case, the product is 'YOU.' Your tag should be short, original, and memorable. It's your last shot at making an impression.

As you're watching television, what gets you to watch a commercial? More often than not, it's the first line, the hook. It grabs your attention, forcing you to listen with interest. The very last line of the commercial, the tag, leaves you remembering everything you heard. In many national spots, the tag is often the slogan for the product's current campaign. It should make you want to run out and try that product.

EXERCISE #8

Using your notebook, write down five fun and interesting opening comments to use as your hook or handle. Take your time. Next, write down five fun and interesting choices for your tag. *You want to leave them remembering you.*

One in a Million . . .

Understand this, if you are fortunate enough to get a meeting with an agent or manager, he or she has most likely met with hundreds, if not thousands of other actors in their career. If you are fortunate enough to get an audition, it's likely that the casting director has seen hundreds of other actors that week. When you leave your audition, your two minutes of brilliance will be lost in a sea of videotape and your picture will disappear into a pile three feet high—**unless you stand out**.

What will make you stand out? What is it that will get your picture dog-eared on the corner, or set in a different pile? The answer is simple. It's you. It's you being you, not you pretending to be the person that you think they want you to be. After a meeting, you want casting directors to remember you and want to bring you in for a read. Agents and managers should be excited about the prospects and possibilities of representing you.

> *"For meetings and generals, an actor should come prepared to talk*
> *about themselves. Make me become interested in them. If they are not*
> *excited about their career or future, why should I be? Have some*
> *stories or anecdotes ready . . . so I don't have to do all the work."*
> **Rosemary Welden, CSA, casting director**
> **L.A.**

INTERVIEWING AGENTS AND MANAGERS

With all of the time and hard work devoted to getting meetings with agents and managers, it's easy to lose sight of the fact that you're the one doing the hiring. You're hiring them. You are assembling your team. You're going to be paying them, not the other way around.

> *"It's important to make sure the agent is licensed by the Board of*
> *Labor. The agent should also be SAG and AFTRA franchised. An*
> *actor should follow their instincts and go with the agent they feel*
> *most comfortable with. It's also a good idea to ask around and find*
> *out what type of reputation the agency has."*
> **Charity Marquis, agent**
> **Osbrink Models & Talent, L.A.**

When meeting with agents and managers, it's important for you to ask questions. Don't be shy. These are the people that will be advising you on your career. These are the people that will be promoting and selling you. They will have a great deal of influence over you and your career. It's important for you to trust them, and for you both to see eye to eye. Having representation means you have someone on your team, and playing on the same team requires working together. For a team to be successful, teamwork is a must. A team is two or more people working together towards a common goal. So, it's not only okay to ask questions, it's imperative for your success.

REPRESENTATION: OFFERS AND CONTRACTS

If an agent or manager offers you representation or expresses an interest in representing you, it's okay to take time to consider the offer. Remember, your company is hiring this distributor to distribute your product. Make sure they have answered all of your questions. This is an important step and they will understand if you need a day or two to make your decision. In fact, they will probably be even more eager to sign someone so professional.

"Actors should feel in their gut that they have met the right agent.
Do your homework, so you know the caliber of agent you are meeting
and then let all that go, as the perfect agent for you will be the one who
you connect with, not the one your friends say is the one you should be
with. Other actors and many people in the business give advice that is
not based on full information, so you need to trust your own instincts.
Remember that going to one of the 'biggies' is not necessarily the answer.
Many actors go to the bigger agencies and just sit there or get out on
lots of roles they are not ready for and are never seen on the growth
roles that they need to build the skills, the experience, and the contacts."
Josh Schiowitz, agent
Schiowitz, Clay, Ankrum & Ross, Inc., L.A.

"The number one thing I look for in a potential client is dedication. They
(actors) should look for an agent that is established, has a good reputation
and is just as dedicated."
Jack Scagnetti, agent
Jack Scagnetti Talent Agency, L.A.

Signing On The Dotted Line . . .

Agents will often want what is called a 'handshake' agreement. They will send you out to get feedback from casting directors. For all intents and purposes, they are sending you out as their client. No SAG agreement is signed until you have gone through a trial period. This is actually a good thing for both of you.

Managers, however, will ask for a management agreement, and most agreements will be for three to five years. Why? Because managers spend their time and resources developing you and helping you create your *image*. Developing an 'unknown' is time consuming. It takes the first year or two to get you established, and to build your resume and demo reel so an agent has something to sell. The manager and agent will work together. As we have discussed, a manager does all the things the agent hasn't the time for: setting up generals, networking, grooming, follow-up and hand-holding. The agent is working on *getting you auditions*, and the manager is working on *getting you ready to audition*.

SCENE TWELVE
AUDITIONS AND AUDITIONING

ACTORS AND AUDITIONS

As your career progresses, you will find that you will encounter many types of auditions and will be asked to do many different things while auditioning. An audition for theater will be much different from a TV or film audition. A commercial audition will be much different from a voice-over audition. Depending upon the type of project, casting directors will be looking for different things. They will either be looking for a particular look, voice, talent, or skill, or they might be looking for some combination. Being professional, developing your skills as an actor, and developing and implementing the right marketing plan will increase the odds that they are looking for you.

"Meetings are a 'get to <u>know</u> you'. Auditions are a 'get to <u>show</u> you."
Bradford Hill, producer/director
Commercial Works, L.A.

The subject of *auditioning* requires more than one or two chapters. The subject alone warrants an entire book of it's own, and will be the subject of my next work. What I want to do in this chapter is to give you an overview of the auditioning process and the various types of auditions actors encounter. We will discuss the *'Do's and Don'ts'* of auditioning, as well as audition preparation. I would also hope that you gain some insight as to what various casting directors, producers, and directors look for in auditions. Audition techniques will be discussed in the following chapter. Let's scratch the surface.

THE AUDITION PROCESS

When a production company is ready to begin casting, they prepare a *breakdown*. A *breakdown* consists of all the production's relevant information, such as title, producing company, addresses and phone numbers, as well as the names of the casting director, director, producers, and any talent attached. Submission deadlines and the start dates of auditions and principle photography, as well as union affiliations, if any, would also be listed. A breakdown also includes the story line, as well as a brief description of the roles available. Once prepared, the casting director sends the breakdown out to services such as Castnet and Breakdown Services. In many instances, the breakdown is prepared by this service, as well. They 'break' the script down by characters or available roles, including character descriptions and any notes that have been sent by the casting director. These services will then send out the breakdown to all subscribing agents and managers via fax, messenger or the Internet. It is from these breakdowns that agents and managers submit their talent for particular roles.

Breakdowns usually don't include leading roles, or *principles*. The production will deal directly with agents when making offers to the principles, or *stars*. They are most likely known actors. There are exceptions. Sometimes a production will want a new face, and lower budget films don't have the money for name talent. In these instances, the leading roles will appear on the breakdown.

Breakdowns and Scripts

Other than from your subscribing agent(s) or a manager, breakdowns are not readily available for actors. If you can get your hands on them, you will find a wealth of information that will aid you in getting the role. Once you've booked an audition, find out if your agent, manager, or the casting office will fax or e-mail you a copy of the breakdown.

If you do manage to get breakdowns, remember, most casting directors want to receive agent submissions only. To avoid being submitted for roles for which they are probably not right, most agents prefer that their clients not submit themselves. If you're up for a role in a film, ask if you can get a copy of the script; if no copies are available, ask when would be a convenient time for you to go to the office and read an office copy?

This industry is highly competitive. Unless you're reading for a lead role, obtaining a script can be nearly impossible, but it doesn't hurt to ask. Most productions are very secretive when it comes to scripts. It has become common practice for scripts to be numbered and distributed to only a select few on an 'as needed' basis. Those receiving scripts are asked to sign for them and agree not to distribute any portion of them. Some productions will print their scripts on colored paper, which makes it virtually impossible to photocopy.

Breakdown Services offers a service called *'Screenplay Online.'* When a client is up for a sizeable role, the casting director can give the agent a 'script code.' With this code, and a small fee, agents can download the script to give to their client.

Check Your Messages!

We have discussed having a separate business line, answering service, or voice mail for your business. You should also have a pager or cell phone, as well as e-mail. It's important to check your messages and e-mail frequently. Many times your messages will be timely, requiring an immediate response.

Write it Down!

When you get calls for auditions and meetings, you'll want as much information as possible. Therefore, you must be ready with the right questions. It might be a good idea to keep a checklist by the phone. Don't rely on memory; write everything down and then read it back. If you are driving, either pull over immediately or call back as soon as you can pull over. Don't be distracted; your audition information is too important. Make sure all of the information is clear and that you understand it. You can also have your agent or manager fax or e-mail you all of the information along with the breakdown.

Keep the following questions handy, so you'll remember to ask.

Things you need to know:
- What day, date, and time?
- What's the name of the project?
- Who will I be reading for?
- Names of the CD, director, producers?
- Address with suite number, cross streets, and parking info?
- Phone number?
- Is it a commercial, sitcom, soap, episodic, or film?
- Will the director be there?
- Will I be taped?
- When will sides be available?
- Where can I get the sides? Fax service? Internet?
- When will a full script be available?
- Can I get a copy of the breakdown?
- What should I wear?
- Any pointers?
- Should I get a coach?
- Name of the role?

Once you have all of the information you will need, look up the casting director, director, and producers in your database or reference material. Find out any useful information that will help you during your audition or meeting.

On Your Side . . .

'Sides' are photocopies of the scenes or portions of the scenes you will be asked to read at your audition. Once you're cast, sides refer to photocopies of the scenes or portions of the scenes that are being filmed or taped on a given day of production.

Many years ago, troupes of actors would travel from village to village. They would set up camp and put on shows for several nights. Each night, the entire town or village would attend their performance. So each night, they would be expected to perform a different show for the same audience. Because the actors couldn't possibly memorize that much material, they would pull their scripts apart and use each page as a mini 'cue-card' during performances. The actors would strategically place script pages all around the set. They would tack a page to the *side* of the door, the *side* of the desk, the *side* of the flat, the *side* of the chair.

That's how pages pulled from a script became known as *sides*.

The sooner you can get your hands on your sides, the better. You want to have as much time as possible to prepare for your audition. The question is, how soon and where can you get the sides. Most likely, your agent or manager will get a copy to you via fax, messenger, Internet, or have them available for you to pick up at their office. Most of the time, casting directors will make sides available at their offices, either the morning of or the day before your audition. If you do pick your sides up at the casting office, get in and get out. Don't be a nuisance. You may also want to consider joining Showfax or Castnet to have your sides sent to you via fax or the Internet. Castnet: **www.castnet.com,** Showfax: **www.showfax.com.**

THE AUDITION:

The audition is not the time to be nervous; the time to be nervous is when you don't have an audition. During an audition, remember everyone in the room wants you to be successful. The casting director has spent hours and hours going through piles of submissions, and the director and producers are on a tight time schedule. They want you to be right for the role. They're on your side.

A casting director is usually on a fee basis, so if it takes two weeks or two months, the fee for casting is the same. Casting, like all trades in this industry, is also a freelance profession. And, you're 'only as good as your last job.' They hope one of their choices is 'dead on' and will please the director and producers. For a casting director, there's nothing worse than having to go back to 'first calls' after you've taken your choices to the director and producer(s). They really are on your side.

Take Control!

When you walk into an audition, take control of the space. Make the room your own. Acknowledge everyone in the room. Move **your** chair if you need to, have a good sight line with the casting director, and make sure everyone else in the room can see your face. Be comfortable and take your time. Have a picture and resume ready, even though you know they already have one. Have your sides ready. Don't think of the things you can't control; go with the things you can. Show them who you are from the moment you walk in the door.

> " . . . *your child is the professional. For an audition, you (parents) take on the role of chauffeur. You drive, you sign the paperwork, and you become your child's greatest silent cheerleader. Do not be pushy or aggressive with casting directors. Even if you have had a bad day yourself, do not show attitude, anger, or depression; your attitude toward your child will affect your child's audition.*

Never tell a child that he/she has to do a good job; that will place more pressure on the child and cause difficulty within the audition process."
Martin Weiss, manager
ETS Management, L.A.

Who Are You?

Remember, during your interview or audition, the casting director, producer, and director are trying to get an idea of 'who you are.' Therefore, when you cold-read, just being yourself is important. Don't try to audition the concept of the character because your concept and your perception of the character may not be theirs. Often during a read, a casting director will say, "Just talk to me. Don't act. Be yourself." This is exactly what they mean. How can you be yourself and be creative? If you were the character in that given situation, how would you react? How would you respond? I'll go further into the audition process in the next chapter and in more depth in the next book.

You Are the Role

Many of you have experience in the theater. There is a distinct difference between performing on stage and performing in front of the camera. In the theater, the actor becomes the role. You spend weeks in rehearsal becoming that role. But, when working in front of a camera, the role becomes you.

The role is your height, your coloring, your background, your age, your experiences and your thoughts. The role is **you** saying those lines. If you were the character in this given situation, how would you react and how would you respond? If you have the role of a 'restrained' person that keeps all of their emotions locked up inside, and in real life you are just the opposite, how would you play that role? If you are not the type that restrains and keeps feelings in check, you would probably yell and throw something. How do you take that role and be yourself? Put yourself in a public place, such as a restaurant. Feel like you just want to scream and throw a plate—but don't.

Walk into an audition and share yourself, trust your impulses and your choices, and accept the premise. (I will discuss choices in the following chapter.) Reactions for camera become more important than the dialogue. *A film actor gets paid for all the things he thinks and feels, but doesn't say.* Theater tells a story in words, as does TV. Film tells a story with pictures. Holly Hunter won an *Oscar* for one line in *The Piano*. No actor has ever won a *Tony* for one line on stage. For theater, it's about dialogue; for film, it's about non-dialogue.

If I took a hundred people and lined them up on the side of a street to witness a car accident, they would all have different reactions. No one could come along and say one reaction was more honest than another. A reaction cannot be judged. On camera, acting is reacting. It's visual. When you're watching a film and leave your seat to get popcorn, what's the first thing you say when you come back? "What did I miss?" Because what you missed was visual—moving pictures.

If, on the other hand, you are watching TV at home and get up to make popcorn, you won't miss much. They will repeat the 'plot line' and you'll be able to catch up. TV tells stories with words. Theater is the same way. Theater and TV are closely related in that they are both performed in 'real time' or 'living time.' In the theater, if you leave your seat, you'll be able to catch up when you return, as they too will repeat the dialogue. Now, this doesn't mean that reactions aren't important in television. Reactions can be even more important in TV because of the small screen. Television actors are at a disadvantage. In a TV 'close-up,' the actor is robbed of the use of his hands and body to get his feelings across. Because of the smaller screen, it is more difficult for TV actors to convey emotions with their eyes. Film actors have the luxury of a big screen for subtle reactions.

THE COLD READ

After you have knocked the socks off the casting directors, agents, or managers with a monologue and a lot of charm, hopefully you will be asked to cold read. They have just seen your rehearsed performance, now they may want to see if you are natural, if you can take direction, and if you have that same 'spark' with their particular script. The cold read is the way the business works. Don't try to change it, **deal with it** and **enjoy it.** This is the process for being cast, represented and/or managed.

A *cold read* is 'cold' in the sense that you are not given much time with your sides or the chance to 'warm up' to the role. It is essential for every actor to learn and understand the technical aspects of cold reading. You must learn to become comfortable holding your sides or script. You need to become proficient with *sight-reading*.

> *"Cold reading skills are extremely important for both children and adults. Scripts are constantly being rewritten during the filming of both television and film. You need to be prepared to handle new pages at any given moment. Many times auditions will come in at the last moment with perhaps an hour or two to prepare, cold read skills will give you the advantage in any audition, especially if they ask you to read new pages."*
> **Jan Brown, manager**
> **JDS Management, L.A.**

Hold On!

Before you get your first meeting or audition, you will need to learn and practice holding a script during cold-reads. Below are some exercises to help you.

Holding Sides and Scripts:

If you're right-handed, hold the script with your left hand, and vice versa. Your other hand is free for gesturing. Now, place the script flat against your chest, under your chin. Without moving your elbow, bring the script down, so you can read it. Your face should be visible; your script shouldn't cover it. This is important, whether you're reading one-on-one without a camera, or if you're being taped.

  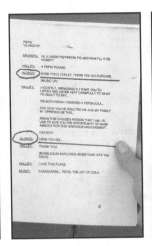

Place script flat against your chest.

Without moving your elbow, bring the script down to read it. Your face should be visible.

Make eye contact and deliver your line..

If the sides are more than one sheet and the sheets are stapled, then take it apart. The reason this is important is that rustling pages are very noisy and will easily be picked up by the microphone. It is also easier to turn the pages if you remove the staples. Turning pages that are stapled is also distracting. The tendency is for people to look at the pages instead of you. Removing staples will make it quieter and easier for you to handle, and won't draw attention away from your face.

Again, if you're right handed, hold the script in your left hand and gesture with your right. The hand that's holding the script never moves. Make your gestures with your free hand, which will prevent you from pulling the focus away from your face with the script and prevent any rustling of the paper. The script should eventually become an extension of your hand.

If you or someone you know owns a video camera, use it to practice your techniques.

When you watch the tape, look to see if your face was covered. If you don't have a camera, practice your cold read techniques in front of a doorknob. The doorknob is the same circumference as a camera lens and it gives you the same emotional input as many casting directors. Nothing!

Clock Watching . . .

Commercial auditioning is direct to the camera lens. You will probably be reading from cue cards and not from your sides. This allows for more eye contact with the lens. During your commercial audition, look at the camera lens as if it were the circumference of a clock. Put your eye contact near the top of the lens—eleven o'clock to one o'clock. If you look at the lower part of the lens, your eyes will appear to be closed, in the middle of the lens, you will appear sleepy. If you look high on the lens, your eyes will look open.

Look right through the camera lens, not right at it. If you look right at it, you will have a 'glazed' look in your eyes. Look through it; try to see your best friend on the other side. Become friends with the camera lens and you will never be intimidated by it. Again, practice with a video camera. Watch yourself. Do you look natural and believable?

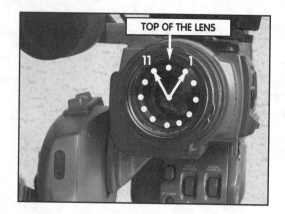
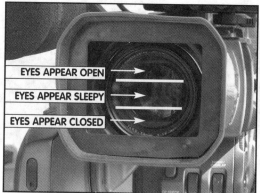

In Sight

Next, you will need to practice *sight-reading*. The better your sight-reading skills become, the more eye contact you will have with the person with whom you're reading.

Memorize your **first** line, and put your thumb on your **second** line. Make eye contact with your scene partner, auditor, or the camera lens and deliver your first line. Hold the eye contact to *receive* their response. This is your *reaction*. Next, drop your eye to your thumb for your next line, then look up and deliver the line. Move your thumb down to the following line, make eye contact, then deliver your line. Maintain eye contact with your partner to, again, receive his line.

Don't speak unless you have eye contact with your scene partner. This is *sight-reading*. You must practice. Your eyes aren't used to looking down, focusing on text, then looking back up to deliver the lines. Practice with scripts, textbooks, newspapers, or even a cereal box. Again, if you have access to a video camera, use it to practice. Watch yourself, and keep practicing until it becomes more natural and less awkward. **Never practice lines or sight-reading in front of a mirror.**

Got Pen?

Always carry a supply of pens and pencils with you at all times. You will need to make notes on your sides, and circle or underline dialogue. Highlighters are also something you should always carry with you. Some actors don't want to highlight; they like to circle their dialogue. I find highlighting leaves you with fewer marks to distract you.

SLATE!

A *'slate'* is your on-camera introduction. Actors slate at the beginning and end of video-taped auditions. Your slate would include your name and a personal salutation. For example: "Hello", my name is John Smith," or "How ya doin'? I'm John Smith." If you are a minor, ask if you should include your age in your slate. For example, "How's it going? My name is John Smith and I'm fourteen."

In a commercial audition situation, you would slate and then likely read from cue cards, directly to camera. For theatrical auditions, if taped, you would slate directly to camera, then establish eye contact with the casting director or reader. Usually, there are no cue cards used in theatrical auditions. This is another opportunity to show off your wonderful sight-reading skills. After your 'taped read' or audition, you may be asked to *'tail-slate.'* For example, at the end of your read, you would say, "Thank you. My name is John Smith."

Even if you have your sides memorized, hold your script. **Never put your script down.** As long as you're holding a script, the auditors expect an *audition*. Once you put the script down, they expect a *performance* and will assume they are seeing your best work.

Slate with Animation!

I'm frequently asked if I think actors should use a slate as an opportunity to show some personality. I say, "Yes." Slate with animation, "Hi, I'm Judy Jones, and I'm looking forward to working with you." Sell it a little bit. Now, some casting directors prefer that you don't do this. They would prefer you just say, "Hi, my name is ____," but why not add some personality to stand out. For example, if you have a younger look, or if you're over eighteen and reading for a teen role, you could say, "Hey, what's up? I'm Joe Smith, and I'm over eighteen." Just make sure to take a moment between your slate and your read. The slate throws off some actors. Don't rush. Take a moment to get back into character.

If you remember one thing at your audition, remember to slate. Imagine the director watching four hours of casting tapes to decide which actors he would like to see for callbacks. He sees you. He loves you, but no slate. Is he going to search through a mountain of pictures to find the face that resembles the one on the video? Or, will you be instantly forgotten? I don't have to answer that, do I?

4 Eyes or 2?

If you wear glasses, take them off to slate. Look into the lens, smile and slate. Introduce yourself with a big smile, and then you can put your glasses back on to read the cue cards or your sides. Now they have both looks on tape and know that once you've memorized your lines, you won't need glasses.

"Take My Picture . . . Please"

Always carry pictures and resumes in your car or in your briefcase. **_Always_**. You never know whom you're going to meet, or whom you'll run into. Even though your agent or manager has already submitted a picture and resume, you still might be asked for another one. There may be someone else in the room who will want one. Remember, when people in the industry want your picture, it's a good thing. Be generous with your photos.

Don't Touch!

Don't touch or move anything on the auditor's desk. I once had an actor in a moment of passion, during his read, take his hand and clear everything off my desk in one great sweeping gesture—and I mean everything: phone, lamp, pictures, files! I was too taken with the mess on the floor to pay any attention to his read. I wanted to strangle him, not cast him.

THEATRICAL AUDITIONS

A theatrical audition is an audition for television (soap, sitcom, episodic, mini series, MOWs), or film. It is an audition for a specific role. The difference between TV and film auditions, usually has to do with how and when you are taped, as well as the number of people in the room.

In a theatrical audition, you will read with someone, most likely the casting director. If your audition is taped, your eye-line is to the person with whom you are reading, not the camera. The only time a theatrical audition is 'direct' to the camera is if you are directed to do so, or when a line is an 'aside' directed to the audience. At those times, you break *'the fourth wall.'*

Four Walls?

'The fourth wall' is an imaginary 'wall' that completes a set. In theater, the fourth wall is the imaginary wall that separates the actor from the audience. For film and television, the fourth wall is the camera. As an audience, we are eavesdropping on the characters. They are not aware we are watching them rob banks, ride bikes, or make love. We see through their walls and into their cars. They can walk or drive toward us, without running us over.

When watching *Friends* or *Kramer*, have you ever wondered what the other side of their apartments looked like? Probably not; we just accept they are there. In films and hour-long dramas on TV, the camera moves around. On *The Practice*, we know what the back of the courtroom looks like; we have seen it. When the camera is facing the front of the courtroom, we accept that it's still there.

When an actor breaks the fourth wall, he is speaking directly to the camera, directly to the audience. Mathew Broderick broke the wall by speaking directly to the audience in *Ferris Bueller's Day Off* and again in *Inspector Gadget*. They break the wall routinely in the TV show *Malcolm in the Middle*. You can also find examples of this in the old Abbott & Costello films.

The 'BOOB TUBE'

Usually, you only have two shots in TV. You will audition once for the casting director and, hopefully, once for the producers. If the casting director knows you and knows your work, he/she can send you right to the producers. This is a good thing. It saves you time, money, and gas, as well as the stress and anxiety of auditioning several times. The down side of going directly to producers is you are missing out on the casting director's input, which can be extremely valuable. If you are going directly to producers, ask your agent or manager to speak with the casting director or arrange for you to speak with the casting director, prior to your audition.

Your first audition for television is, usually, held in the casting director's office and you will not be taped. If there are callbacks, you should expect a taped audition. When you go directly to producers for television, the casting director is going to be reading with you and you will meet the director and producer(s). If they all can't be present, then they will tape the reading.

The 'Silver Screen'

More time is, usually, spent on auditions for films. Television works on a very tight schedule; films don't have the same time constraints, so the process is longer. TV, usually, has a week to cast, whereas films could have four to twelve weeks, depending on the film's budget.

Your first read is with the casting director. You may even have a *'callback'* with the casting director. Depending on how many actors the director wants to see, the casting director will likely narrow their choices to about eight to twenty actors, per role. This is what I refer to as the *'director's call.'* The director is looking for **reaction** and believability.

Some directors like to have a big choice and will see several actors at callbacks. Other directors like to see only a few people. After callbacks, the director picks two or three actors per role to take to the producer. This is what I refer to as the *'producers call.'* This is the first time the actor reads with another actor. At that point, they are looking for **interaction**, the chemistry with other actors.

If you are brought in to read with the star, then you are reading for a *'supporting role'*

. . . hence the term. Can you 'support' the star? Many times, actors lose roles because they look too much like the star. They are too good-looking, not good-looking enough, too tall, too short, same coloring, a better actor than the star, or they just can't hold their own—you know, a variety of reasons.

THE FIRST READ

Prepare your sides well in advance of your call time and practice your sight-reading. Always bring your pictures and resumes with you. Arrive at least thirty minutes before your call time to give you the opportunity to relax and look over the material. Make sure the sides you were given are the same sides you will be auditioning with. Last minute changes happen frequently.

Look over the script; make sure you understand the concept, know how to pronounce all the words, etc. Read it over a couple of times to yourself, then read your own lines out loud, so the sound of your own voice won't throw you. Some actors come out of an audition and start to socialize with the other actors in the waiting room. **Don't let someone else interfere with your preparation time.** Stay focused on what you are there to do. Sign in only when you are ready to audition, and be professional, at all times.

Read Lines—DON'T LINE READ . . .

Parents must remember, it is the child who is the actor. If your child requires coaching, hire a professional. Read lines with your child if they find it helpful, but **do not line read**. Don't encourage your child to mimic the lines the way you would say them. If your child is too young to read, help him memorize his lines, and help with pronunciation. Your help should be devoid of any and all emotion. Again, if your child requires coaching, hire a professional.

"Some parents feel it necessary to tell their children how to state their lines or how to perform. A child's imagination is a wonderful world; once you toss too much of your own reality into that world at an audition, the freshness and innocence that would have otherwise shown your child to be an actor will be lost. In other words, do not line read. If your child needs an acting partner for cold dialogue, play the other part; that still does not mean you should tell your child how to perform his/her role."
Martin Weiss, manager
ETS Management, L.A.

Autographs . . . PLEASE!

Prior to your audition, you must sign in. All auditions have a 'sign-in' sheet. Arriving early is so important. You'll need the time to prepare, and it is good practice to sign in at least fifteen minutes prior to your call time. Most sign in sheets ask for your social security number. I suggest you write in your union membership number instead. If you're non-union, leave it blank. Once you're cast, your agent or manager will give them your personal information. If you're a union actor without representation, check with SAG to verify that the project is a union signatory, prior to giving out any personal information.

"I'm Flexible"

When you walk into the casting director's office, ask, "Do you want to see what I've prepared or is there something specific you are looking for?" This tells the casting director you are **prepared**, you've made **choices**, and you're **flexible**. Most of all, it says you're a **professional**. Many times, casting directors aren't really sure what they're looking for, so they will say, "Yeah, go ahead, let's see what you have."

Well, now you have carte blanche for your own choices, because they just said, "Let's see what you have." However, if they do give you an adjustment, be prepared to follow it. Making that statement is a risk, so you've got to prepare. I know a lot of actors will say, "Would you like to see it differently?" I'll say "Sure," and then they'll do it exactly the same way. Those actors never get the role. Be careful suggesting another take on the read or when asking, "Do you have any adjustments?" You must be able to deliver just that, another take on the read or immediately interpret the adjustment and follow direction.

> *"Be flexible. Have several different ways to read the material, so that if you are asked to go a different way, you have a foundation to rely on."*
> **Rosemary Welden, CSA, casting director**
> **L.A.**

Many times, you will be asked to read material other than the material you have prepared. Often, during the casting process, you may be considered for a role other than the one for which you originally auditioned. If the casting director asks you to read a different scene or for a different role, don't try to wing it. Say, "Why don't I send the next person in while I look over this new scene. That way I won't keep you waiting."

> *"Never do an ice-cold read—always ask for time to prepare."*
> **Diane Hardin, manager**
> **Hardin/Eckstein Management, L.A.**

Only an amateur tries to impress without preparation. Everybody knows a professional actor cannot just pick up a script he's never seen, look at it, and make things happen. You need time; otherwise, they would just pull people off the street and say, "Here, do this."

Once you are ready to begin your audition, if you want to stand or sit, just do it. Be in control. Do your thing. An exception would be a taped audition. You have to stay within the camera's framing. But even then, ask the camera operator, "Will it throw you off if I stand?" Let him decide.

A Nice Exit . . .

When you are finished with your audition, **your *exit* should be nice and clean**. If you ask if there's anything else they would like to see, and the answer is "No," immediately get up, thank them for their time, and *exit*.

If you have done your homework and know a little something about the casting director, this would be a great time to add something personal. You might add, "Nice to meet someone else from Detroit," or something to do with a common interest. This is the time to offer your reel, if you have one. Again, don't expect to get it back and don't ask.

COMMERCIAL AUDITIONS

Commercial auditions are videotaped. You tape once and, probably, only once. During the audition, casting directors will tape many actors. The producers then select the ones they want their client or the ad-agency to see. The ad-agency will, likely, have the producers edit the tape with the actors on it they want their client to see.

You will be expected to fill out a 'stat-card' asking for your sizes, home address and phone, as well as agency contact. This is the exception to the rule, 'Don't give out your personal information.' If a SAG agent has sent you on a SAG commercial audition, it's a safe situation to offer your personal information. Commercial casting works quickly. The production office may need to contact you immediately for wardrobe, set location, or call-time, and not be able to reach your agent. Your agent will be contacted as soon as possible.

They will also take a Polaroid picture, as they want a photo that is untouched and looks like you. It will be a close-up. So smile, relax, put your left shoulder forward, and face front. This will help give the photo some dimension.

"Where's the Beef?"

Be on time. There are very few 'cattle calls' today. Most auditions are by appointment. For commercials, casting directors will often group people together by type or role. In many cases, they are trying to create the look of a family and will group by age, ethnicity, or coloring. By not being on time, you throw off the audition tape. If you're auditioning for the role of 'Ken' and you arrive while they're taping the role of 'Mary,' you're not only being inconsiderate and unprofessional, but you may not be put on tape. If you are put on the tape, you'll be out of sequence and run the risk of not being considered. You will have to bank on someone remembering to fast-forward the tape when they are considering your role. Don't count on it.

Commercial auditions work so fast, there is rarely time to get sides or copy out to actors prior to their auditions. That's why it's imperative to not only be on time, but to arrive early. Arriving early will allow you time to sign in, get your Polaroid taken, fill out the stat-sheet, and study your sides or copy. And, if you are part of a grouping, you will have an opportunity to read and interact with your group.

If a commercial requires dialogue, you will most likely do a cold read. Other commercial auditions, dialogue or not, may require improvisations or pantomime. They are looking for spontaneity, personality, and fun. Most commercial auditions requiring dialogue will use cue cards. Again, this is so the talent will be able to look directly into the camera and not at the script, since the actors will usually have just a few minutes to prepare.

"Pass the vinegar"

As close as my mother and I are—and I have a very close family—when we go out to lunch we do not discuss feminine hygiene. Commercials aren't always realistic; most are somewhat unrealistic. Commercial style is bigger than life. We smile too much and we're too happy. The public is conditioned to that 'better than the best,' 'new and improved,' and 'bigger than life' commercial style.

If you woke up to find a lumberjack doing your dishes, you would call the police. If your margarine started talking, you would probably call your doctor. In commercials, we just accept these things. We are used to them. When we watch someone eating cereal in a commercial, we accept his or her euphoria

Although the majority of commercials are bigger than life, the style of the ***commercial delivery*** is natural and believable. So, how can you make 'bigger than life' natural and believable? Put yourself in a 'heightened state of emotion.' It's not good, it's ***great***! You're not just happy, you're ecstatic—but it's got to be genuine. Every commercial audition has got to be genuine and sincere. The viewing audience knows immediately if you are faking it! And so will the client.

SMILE!

Commercials for the most part are light and bright, positive, uplifting and cute. At one time, the style for most commercials was way 'over the top,' but not any more. Today, many commercials are natural, with everyday, real people. Keep it believable, be yourself, maintain energy and **smile**! Remember, commercial actors are salespeople, and you can't sell anything if you don't smile.

Practice smiling as you speak. In most commercials, that's what you'll have to do. When auditioning for a spokesperson, the only time you shouldn't smile is if you're selling cemetery plots. Talking with a smile may feel forced. The muscles in your cheeks may feel tense. It takes time. Practice smiling every time you talk on the phone. Try placing a small mirror near your phone. While you're talking, you can watch your mouth to see if you're smiling or not. People will immediately recognize something different. People will get the impression that something good is happening in your life. With practice, it will eventually become easier and more natural to speak with a smile.

WARDROBE PROPS AND MAKEUP

The breakdown will give details on the type and personality of each of the characters. They may even provide a little back-story. That information will help you in deciding what to wear. For example, if the character is a proper, conservative woman, you're not going to wear a low-cut blouse and a short, tight skirt with a slit. You're going to dress conservatively.

"I always say GAP. Nice pastels are great on camera! You don't want to wear clothes that speak louder than you. Believe me when I say, sometimes the clothing overwhelms the actor. Don't make a statement in the audition, make an impression! Always, wear an outfit that doesn't detract from you . . . the actor."
Judy Belshe, casting director
Judy Belshe Casting, L.A.

"Their agent should be telling them what to wear, if they don't have an agent, use common sense. Dress nice. No shorts or tank tops unless the role calls for it. If meeting for a general interview, then casual is good."
Brien Scott, casting director
L.A.

What To Wear?

I don't believe in costumes. If you are a man going in for the role of a policeman or a military officer, just wear a suit. We behave differently in suits, just as we do in uniforms. We walk differently—we just do. If you're auditioning for the role of a nun, a turtleneck and long skirt would be appropriate. I think your wardrobe should be characteristic of the role.

"Talent should really only come in costume if requested. However, it is necessary sometimes. But for the most part, the 'clothing idea' of the character will do for me on the first call. Then if you get a callback, I may ask you change what you are wearing. Example: if you are coming in for the part of an airline pilot then a nice dark blazer, tie and shirt would work."
Judy Belshe, casting director
Judy Belshe Casting, L.A.

When auditioning for an extreme role like a biker, jeans and a leather or denim jacket would be fine. Don't show up looking like you rode your 'Hog' for five hundred miles. Always go in clean and well groomed. If the role requires a rougher look, don't shave the night before. Keep it simple.

" . . . maybe a bit of the costume (is appropriate), if it helps the actor perform. But, to come in a major costume is a waste of time. . . . for a nun, the wimple is fine, but dressing in the whole garb is silly. I always discourage props. Props should be supplied by casting."
James F. Tarzia, CCDA, casting director
James Tarzia Casting, L.A.

"For the standard audition, an actor should dress for casual comfort, not to impress. However, casual does not mean holes in t-shirts and tattered jeans. For young children, play clothes will suffice. For older children, school clothing is fine. DO NOT wear shirts with busy patterns or logos."
Martin Weiss, manager
ETS Management, L.A.

If you're a minor, dress the way you normally do. Young girls should wear very little to no makeup, with their hair worn off the face. Children should avoid jewelry, especially earrings that dangle; you're better off wearing studs.

"Young actors should always dress their age or younger, Jeans,
T-shirt, tennis shoes; nothing with a logo or writing on it, no prints
or jewelry. Very natural hair—a few highlights."
Judy Savage, agent
The Savage Agency, L.A.

Knowing that most auditions are videotaped, dress appropriately. Avoid black, white, and brightly colored shirts or blouses. Black pants or slacks are okay. Stay away from shirts and blouses with busy patterns or prints. Avoid any jewelry that moves, dangles, or makes noise. Women should wear their hair off the face. The face is what's important. Avoid any make-up that will distract or draw attention away from your face. Be comfortable. If you feel self-conscious wearing revealing clothing, then don't. If you're not comfortable in high heels, don't wear them. If you're not comfortable, you will not audition well, and you won't get the job.

"Makeup is for models and monsters. An actress should impress with
her talent and skills. A blossoming young adult may wish to accentuate
her look with highlights, but do not assume that a face full of makeup
is going to book the job. Look and act human, not plastic."
Martin Weiss, manager
ETS Management, L.A.

"If a girl doesn't need make-up, then I don't care how old she is,
don't wear a lot—maybe a little blush and lip gloss. Being a children's
agent, I want my clients to look young and fresh, not fake and made up.
Only in a few instances is a lot of make-up called for, for an audition."
Carolyn Thompson-Goldstein, agent
Amsel, Eisenstadt & Frazier, Inc., L.A.

"If it Ain't Broke . . . "
For callbacks, you'll always want to wear the same outfit you auditioned in originally. In your appointment book, computer or PDA, make a note about what you were wearing and how you wore your hair. It will be helpful for your callback. Casting directors often remember actors by what they wore.

There are " . . . actors that show up for the first interview wearing clothes that fit the role, and then get called back and wear something completely opposite. They should write down in a journal exactly what they wore and do it again. . . . if you go to the first interview with a beard and come to the callback clean-shaven, you have just ruined the first impression, which is the reason you were called back."
Brien Scott, casting director
L.A.

On one particular casting session, after a long day of auditions, the director remembered the girl in the red dress. That's whom he wanted to cast. Although he needed to have callbacks, he was set on the girl in the red dress. At the end of callbacks, he asked me what happened to the girl in the red dress. "Why didn't she show?" Well, she did show, only she wore a blue suit. He was so focused on the red dress, he hadn't noticed her and he cast someone else. In the blue suit, she just didn't impress him in the same way. **Always wear the same thing to call backs.** If you're called back, they liked what they saw and the choices you made. Don't make changes unless you are directed to do so.

The Lucky Shirt

I think every actor should go out and buy one outfit that makes them feel absolutely fabulous and keep it for auditions. You know how there are certain things in your closet you put on and you just feel great, and there are other things you put on and you're just "Ugh!" You think "I never bought this," or "Someone must have given it to me." I have a lot of those. They are too tight or too small; you're just not comfortable. You need something you are really comfortable in, something you feel fabulous wearing. Most men have a favorite shirt. One man I know has a cream-colored shirt and he just loves it. Whenever he's nervous about an audition, I say, "Wear that shirt." There's something about a man wearing a shirt or sweater he feels great in. It's the same with a woman. Just recently, a friend of mine gave me a sweater for my birthday, when I looked at it, I thought, "God, I'll never wear this." Well, I have worn it at least once a week since I got it. I absolutely love it. It feels great and I get so many compliments.

Props?

Don't over prop. It's distracting, and will draw attention away from you. Very simple props are fine in a cold read audition, providing these are props you would have or carry with you anyway, such as, your wallet, purse, keys, money, jacket, sweater, or cell phone (turned off, of course).

I once had an actor come into my office for an audition. He proceeded to set down a boom box. Out of his large dance bag came wineglasses, a wine bottle, and flowers in a box. He then took out another shirt and changed. He combed his hair, and as he pushed the button to start the music, the scene began. I was so caught up in watching him 'set dress' and 'do wardrobe,' I never paid any attention to what he was saying or how he was saying it. He did nothing but 'pull focus' away from himself. If there were a list of all the 'don'ts,' he hit every one of them in a matter of minutes.

TO DO AND NOT TO DO

✔ Don't be late. In fact, arrive fifteen minutes early.

✔ If it is necessary for you to be late, DON'T. Don't be late, ever.

✔ Never make excuses for tardiness. In an emergency, have your agent or manager call and let casting know that your last appointment ran later than expected.

✔ Don't ever apologize. Actors, being fragile and insecure, have a tendency to apologize for their very being.

✔ Always try to maintain eye contact and conversational dialogue with your reader or interviewer.

✔ Be prepared for adjustments. It means they like you.

✔ Carry your tools with you. Always have extra pictures and resumes, as well as any demo-reels, voice-tapes, or your portfolio with you, at all times.

✔ Don't sign in until you're ready to walk into the room. That is your indication that you are now ready to audition.

✔ Enter and exit your audition like a professional.

✔ Dress appropriately.

✔ Always carry pens, pencils, glasses, and a highlighter. If you forget a pen, borrow or steal one before your audition. Don't borrow the casting director's.

✔ During the audition, don't touch anything in the room that doesn't belong to you, except your chair and the doorknob.

✔ Don't smoke. If you must, do it out of sight, not in front of the office. It doesn't look good.

SCENE THIRTEEN
AUDITION TECHNIQUES

BASIC TRAINING

Where and with whom you train will influence how you approach and prepare material. You may choose to adopt a technique of one of the masters, your coach, or a combination of all the above. What I would like to share with you in this chapter will be some simple guidelines that will help you prepare for an audition, no matter what techniques you adopt.

As I've said before, it would take an entire book to properly discuss audition techniques. This is a book on *marketing*, and one of the most important aspects of marketing yourself as a professional actor is presenting yourself professionally, always. Whether you're a seasoned pro or new to this business, you don't want to look like an amateur. One sure-fire way to look amateurish is to have poor auditioning skills.

AUDITION TECHNIQUES 101

The audition is the most creative part of the casting process, and the most fun. This is the actor's opportunity to be creative, make choices, and take risks. This is the time to put all of that wonderful training to use. Once you are cast, it's the director who gets to be creative. So have fun!

Enjoy being yourself. **Don't Act . . . React**. Share your thoughts and feelings, and just have fun. If you are simply reacting and responding as you do with your friends and family, then your own personality will come out. That is just what this industry is looking for.

THEATRICAL TECHNIQUES

You have prepared yourself, you're familiar with the material, and you have made choices. But, you have based most of your choices on the written words of the scene. When cold reading, the other character's lines suddenly come alive. You're hearing them for the first time. The other person's choices may be completely different from what you had thought they might be. Don't just listen to what is being said. Listen to how it is being said. Listen to how the lines are being delivered.

Listen ☆ Digest ☆ React ☆ Respond

Acting is reacting. Don't rush. Take your time. When reading with someone, it's important that you listen and actually hear what he or she is really saying. Take the time to digest it. Listen, digest, react, and then respond. Actors don't take turns delivering lines—that's not acting. The end of your scene partner's line is not your cue to start speaking.

Listen

Actively listen. Listen to what is being said, and what *is not* being said. What choices is the other actor making, or not making? Are you in agreement, or disagreement? Are you excited, disappointed, or angered by what is being said? Eye contact is so important. Our emotions show not only on our faces, but, in our eyes as we listen. This is what the camera wants. What the camera wants is what the casting director wants. Trite, but true . . . "Eyes are the windows of your soul." Always keep the window open!

Digest

You're listening. You hear your scene partner's lines. You hear the words, but do you know what is really being said? Find the sub-text. What is the speaker really saying? Is he being smug, sarcastic, or condescending? How does what was said make you feel? Do you care? If you care, do you want that known? Will you be honest, or mask your emotions? Take a second to digest what is being said.

React

Remember, *film and television actors are paid for what they think, feel, and don't say*. Many directors and established actors will want to cut dialogue from scripts. Certain things are best said visually. Film and television are visual mediums. As a viewing audience, we want to see how characters react to what is being said. It is our nature to be sympathetic and empathetic. We put ourselves in the place of the character that's listening. We identify and relate to those reactions. This is especially true in films.

In film, the camera will often stay on the character that is reacting to what's being said, rather than the speaker. In television, the camera will usually stay on the speaker and then cut to the reaction of other characters. Either way, it's the reaction that is important. The next time you are catching the latest film at the multiplex or enjoying your favorite TV show at home, be aware of where the camera lens is focused. Is it focused on the speaker or the listener?

Respond:

This is the tricky part. Breathing life and believability into the writer's work, is the actor's responsibility. You must bring your own sparkle and spontaneity to the script. During an audition, casting directors and directors are looking and hoping for believability. This is a personality business. Each actor has a different personality and will bring a different nuance to the role. Ask yourself, if you were the character in that given situation, how would you react? How would you respond?

What are you feeling when you say your line? What is the **sub-text** of what you are saying? What is your objective? Responses should feel spontaneous. For the most part, the actual words you are saying are irrelevant. Have you ever watched a foreign film without subtitles or a movie on TV with the volume turned down? You can, usually, get an idea of what they are saying and feeling without hearing the words. Remember, it's not what you are saying; it is how you are saying it.

If you place your hand on a hot burner, it's going to burn and hurt. In real life, you don't leave it on the hot burner and say, "Gee, that's hot." You immediately pull your hand away, scream, and then say "_____!!!!!" We react first. If you were told you'd won the lottery or that a loved one was in danger, words wouldn't immediately start spewing from your mouth. You would digest what's being said, react to what you're hearing, and then you would respond.

CHOICES

Make choices when you break down a script. Your choices should be interesting and unexpected. It's always good to go with the unexpected, because people remember the unexpected. And in auditions, you always want to be remembered, especially in that first read . . . you want a callback.

Your choices don't necessarily have to come from the script. For instance, if your character is nervous and uneasy, try concentrating on having to go to the bathroom. On camera, this will create the effect of being nervous and uneasy. Be creative and use your imagination. Draw from your past experiences, both good and bad. Actors are called upon to portray many types of characters with varying backgrounds and goals. More often than not, actors lack the actual knowledge and experience of the characters they play. That's why it's called acting.

Many actors have experienced the joy of having children and the pain of divorce. If you haven't, draw from your own joyful or painful emotions and experiences. While there are probably several actors who have experienced war, and possibly one or two that have traveled in space, I would wager that no actor has battled a dragon or traveled in time. If space travel and dragon slaying were casting prerequisites, sock-puppets and children would monopolize all of the work. Actors make choices, and choices come from within. Choices make roles believable.

"The actors that I remember are the ones who truly brought themselves into character . . . forgot stage directions, didn't try to shrink their personality into the role, but expanded themselves to include the persona so that I was left with the memory of a real living, breathing, exciting character."
Rosemary Welden, CSA, casting director
L.A.

SCRIPT PREPARATION

Here are some things to think about when you're preparing for an audition. From the very first read, allow the circumstance to affect you. If you were the character in this given circumstance, how would you react? What does the situation do to you? Break the scene down by identifying the *'pre-text,' 'sub-text,' 'objective,'* and *'after-text.'* Every scene has a beginning, middle, and an end. This is a simple way of saying *'moment before,' 'in the moment,'* and *'moment after.'*

Pre-Text ⊃ Sub-Text ⊃ Objective ⊃ After-Text

Pre-Text: 'Pre' means prior or before. Pre-text is before text, what happened or was said prior to the beginning of your scene. Pre-text is back history, 'the moment before,' 'prior life,' or whatever your acting coach calls it. It is the 'life before' the first line.

Sub-Text: Sub-text is what you're thinking, regardless of what you're saying. It's what is *really* being said. Being 'in the moment'—the emotion between the lines. Are you saying one thing, but mean another? You might say to a woman, "I love your dress," when in fact, you think it's hideous. Sub-text can make the things that you do, feel, and say more colorful. It's not what you say, but how you say it. How would you say, "I love your dress," while feeling jealous that she looks so much better in that dress than you would? How would you say, "I love your dress," and really mean it?

Objective: The objective is what your intention is in a certain situation. It is your *need*. What is your *need* or goal in the scene? What are your *intentions*? What do you need to have happen? What are you trying to accomplish? For example, are you trying to 'save the day,' 'get the girl,' or 'win the big game?'

After-Text: After-Text is what you're left thinking and feeling after the last line . . . the *'moment after';* your reaction to what was just said, your thoughts after the conversation. For example, you may be thinking, "I should never have said that," "That didn't come out right," or "I can't believe this is happening."

COMMERCIAL TECHNIQUES

In preparing for your commercial audition, I recommend using the *'W's,'* I'm not sure who started using the W's first, but they are generally known in the acting community as a theatrical audition tool. I prefer them as a commercial tool, as does Joan See, author of *Acting in Commercials*. Shown here is my own variation of the *W's*. Most acting teachers develop their own variations of acting tools and techniques.

Use the W's as a tool to breakdown commercial copy. Don't rush when answering the questions. Properly preparing for an audition takes time. Professional actors understand the importance of being prepared. **Develop a routine now; bad habits are hard to break.** Only amateurs and the unemployed rush the preparation process.

When talking directly to camera, you are talking to one person, not millions of TV viewers. Talking to an audience of one makes commercials feel more intimate. TV viewers should feel like the spokesperson is talking only to them. Think of your best friend as the person to whom you are speaking. Our best friends make us comfortable and at ease. We trust and are able to confide in our friends. Viewers should feel like a friend is letting them in on some important and valuable information, not a salesman looking for a commission.

The W's

W ho are you talking to?
W hat are you doing?
W hen are you doing it?
W here are you?
W hy are you doing it?

WHO are you talking to?	Be specific. Who are they? What's their relationship to you?
WHAT are you doing?	What is the event or activity? Are you riding a horse? Are you sitting in a dental chair?
WHEN are you doing it?	When is the event happening? What time of day? Is it morning, afternoon, or night? Is it past your normal bedtime? Is it time for lunch?
WHERE are you?	Are you at home? Are you at school? Your body language will

	be affected by your environment. Be aware of the snowfall and feel the cold air.
WHY are you doing it?	Why are you telling your friend? Give yourself a reason to do what you do. Create a reason for telling your friend about this product.

The following is an example of what commercial copy looks like. It is from an actual Pepsi spot. Using the W's, practice breaking the copy down. Try reading it once before and again after you prepare the material. Do you see a difference?

Have fun! Commercials should be fun to do and fun to watch! Take risks and use your imagination. Be natural in an exaggerated state. In other words, don't just be pleased, be excited!

Pepsi: "Alonzo's"

GRANDPA: Hi. A large pepperoni pie and what'll it be honey?

HALLEY: A Pepsi please.

ALONZO: Sure thing Curley. There you go Cupcake.

(Music Up)

HALLEY: (Quietly, menacingly) I want you to listen and listen very carefully to what I'm about to say . . .
We both know I ordered a Pepsi-Cola . . .
And now you've insulted me and my family by offering me this . . .
Being the civilized person that I am . . . I'd like to give you the opportunity to make amends for this grievous misjudgment.
Capisci?

ALONZO: Here you go . . .

HALLEY: Thank you.

(Bubblegum explodes—everyone hits the deck)

HALLEY: I like this place.

MUSIC: Bababababa . . . Pepsi. The joy of cola.

What's Your HANDLE?

The W's are great for commercial copy. *'Handles'* and *'buttons'* are great commercial audition tools, as well. The handle, often referred to as the *'hook,'* is an improvised beginning to a scene. It can also be an expression, reaction or gesture. It is an attention grabber. A *handle* is another way for you to show off your wonderful personality. A good *handle* can 'spring board' you into the copy.

Button-Up!

The button, often referred to as a *'tag,'* is an improvised ending to a scene and is used in much the same way as the *handle* or the hook. It's a way of bringing your own personality to a script. It's an exclamation mark to the end of the copy. Your *button* can also be an expression or gesture. Your *button* **must** arise from the situation, the copy.

Here's an example of commercial copy without a handle or button.

Client: XYZ Clothing Store
Title: 'Hot Summer'   :30

Sales Clerk: Summer's almost here, . . . and it's HOT.
And, *XYZ Clothing Store* has all the HOTTEST fashions.
XYZ . . . your summer just got hotter.

Now look at some examples of the same copy with a handle and a button.

Client:	XYZ Clothing Store
Title:	'Hot Summer' :30

Sales Clerk: **WOW!** Summer's almost here . . . and it's HOT.
And, *XYZ Clothing Store* has all the HOTTEST fashions.
XYZ . . . your summer just got hotter . . . **Cool! . . . I mean Hot!**

(or)

Sales Clerk: **Hey Dudes!** Summer's almost here . . . and it's HOT.
And, *XYZ Clothing Store* has all the HOTTEST fashions.
XYZ . . . your summer just got hotter . . . .**Dude**.

(or)

Sales Clerk: **Psssst. Listen up**. Summer's almost here . . . and it's HOT.
And, *XYZ Clothing Store* has all the HOTTEST fashions.
XYZ . . . your summer just got hotter . . . .
You were listening, weren't you?

Make the scene your own. When you shop for clothing, you try on a variety of different sizes, styles, and colors until you find something that works for you and fits you perfectly. Finding that perfect button takes time and thought. You may have to try a number of them before you find the right fit. **By 'buttoning up' the scene, you own it!**

They say the button originated back in Vaudeville. The MC would let the actors know it was time to end an act by telling them to *'button it,'* meaning to close it! The button was a gesture or improvised comment that let the audience know the act was over.

Voice Over Image (VO):

Many commercials are shot without the sound. You'll see the actors interacting with one another. They may be laughing and talking, but you can't hear them. The voice you hear relating their situation or telling you about the car they're driving is that of the **Voice-Over talent**. The voice you hear is recorded separately and independently of the visual image. Music and voice tracks are then added to the visual images, which are of the final steps in completing a commercial. The voice-track is 'laid' over the image, which is where the term *voice-over* came from.

MOS?

Commercials shot this way are called *'MOS,'* meaning they are shot 'without sound.' *MOS* is not just a commercial term, it is used in film and television, as well. Any shot or individual take that does not record 'sync sound' (the sound is in sync with the picture) is referred to as MOS. Most commercials are filmed without sound, simply because they have no need for it in the finished product.

There are certain situations in film, television, and commercials that do require sound, but sync sound cannot be recorded. Examples would be fast or slow motion photography, stunt sequences, and certain special effects. When shooting slow or fast motion, the camera exposes the film more or less than 24 frames per second (24fps is sync film speed). Certain stunt or special effect shots, like explosions and gunfire, are too loud to record. The sounds the audience hears are, usually, added later.

Why isn't it WOS? Well, Hollywood legend has it that a German director of the early 'talkies' by the name of Lothar Mendes was about to shoot a scene without sound, and said, "Ve vill shoot dis mit out sound." It stuck and 'mit out sound' it was!

The 'FUNNIES!'

MOS commercial auditions can be fun. MOS auditions are directed much the same way an improvisation group performs. The actors are given a situation and act it out using their own dialogue and movement. This is called an improvisation. The movement and activity are crucial to the improvisation, as well as the unscripted dialogue. There are usually *storyboards* prepared in advance, which help actors with their preparation. *Storyboards* are sequential, cartoon-like illustrations of the various shots that will comprise the finished commercial.

| *Frame 1* | *Frame 2* | *Frame 3* |

*Copyrighted material reprinted with the permission of **PepsiCo**. Brand: Pepsi, Agency: BBDO, New York.*

Improvise!

The definition *Random House* gives to **improvisation** is, *"1. to compose and perform without previous preparation. 2. to devise or provide from whatever material is available."*

I would add that improvisation skills are essential for the success of any professional actor. I cannot stress enough the need for improvisational training.

The majority of commercials have no dialogue. They rely on the improvisational skills of actors. When auditioning for commercials that do not require dialogue, many actors fail to see the need to prepare for their auditions. The fact is, commercials with no dialogue require more preparation than commercials with dialogue. Failing to recognize this will ultimately be commercial career suicide.

CROW

Viola Spolin, the creator of improvisation, uses what I think is a wonderful technique. She refers to it as *'CROW,'* a process she taught in her improvisational classes. Spolin suggests that you determine the 'WHERE' first. Once your environment is established, character, relationship and objective will follow easily. The following is my version of Spolin's 'CROW.'

C HARACTER:	If you were the character in this given situation, how would you respond? How would you react?
R ELATIONSHIP:	How are you related to those in the scene with you? How are you related to the person to whom you're speaking?
O BJECTIVE:	What do you need to have happen in this scene? What is your desire?
W HERE:	Where are you? How does this specific environment affect your behavior?

Use Your Imagination

Reading with non-actors (casting directors, directors, and producers), or receiving a completely flat read from a scene partner, requires a lot of imagination. Using *'Inner Dialogue'—hearing* lines the way you need to hear them—can help make your reading more believable and conversational. Using Inner Dialogue is using your imagination. Use your imagination as the other actor, reader, or casting director delivers his lines. Hear the interpretation you need to hear for your choices to work within the scene.

Maintain a sense of freedom and spontaneity. Be willing to play and have fun. There is nothing more enjoyable than watching an actor have fun.

Scratching the Surface . . .

We have merely scratched the surface of the various audition techniques available to you. The ones I've discussed are a few of the ones I teach in my cold reading workshops. They are a good start, as well as being 'tried and true.'

ACT VI

YOUR MARKETING PLAN

"Film actors get paid for the things they think and feel,
not what they say."

-Clair

SCENE FOURTEEN
STRATEGIES TACTICS AND PLANS

GETTING STARTED

Those of you who are professional actors and are familiar with how this industry works will find the information in this book easier to digest than those who are new to this business. Those of you who are considering a career in this business will, hopefully, learn from the mistakes of others and begin your career properly, competently, and professionally.

Every actor is different. Every business is different. Every marketing plan is different. Actors differ in age, weight, height, coloring, type, and experience. There are also a number of variables that make each actor unique and will, subsequently, make each actor's marketing plan unique. Variables like time restraints, income, finances, and available resources will influence the way you market yourself.

What time commitments and/or obligations do you have? Do you go to school? Do you have a job? If so, do you work or go to school during the day or at night? Are you married? Do you have a boyfriend or girlfriend? Do you have children? If you are a minor, what sort of time restraints do your parents or guardians have?

What are your financial restraints and/or restrictions? How will you finance your business? Do you have a savings account? Do you have a credit card? If you are a minor, do your parents or guardians have the financial resources to fund you and your career? Your finances will not only determine how you market yourself, but how effectively you market yourself.

What types of resources are available to you? Do you have a car? Do you have a computer? Are any of your friends or family members photographers or acting teachers? Do you already own some of the tools you will need like a phone, pager, answering machine, etc.?

It's Up to You!

I have given you a number of options and suggestions, as well as some creative examples of how other actors have marketed, promoted, and created exposure for themselves. More importantly, I have laid out the basic, but crucial steps to take and the tools you will need to be successful. It is up to you to determine _**how**_ you will market your product.

I can't give you all the answers. Hopefully, you are not just realizing this now. There is no generic plan that will work for everyone. What I can do for you is provide some insight within this industry, guide you in obtaining necessary information and tools, and help with the basic framework and outline of your marketing plan. **Only _you_ can put together _your marketing plan_, and only you can make it work.**

THE RIGHT PLAN

Marketing strategies and tactics are the basic elements of your marketing plan. Your *strategy* or *strategies* are the methods you will use to achieve your goal. Your tactics quantify your desired results. A *tactic* is the method you will use to carry out your strategy. Your *plan* will be the specifics of your tactic, the specific steps you will take to achieve your goal.

If one of your *goals* is to work in television, one *strategy* may be to sign with a good theatrical agent. Your *tactic* might be the use of mailings. Your *plan* would be the *specific steps* you would take when doing your mailings.

For example, your plan may include the following steps:

1. Research and target five theatrical agents.

2. Have new theatrical headshots taken.

3. Update your resume.

4. Compose personalized cover letters.

5. Address, stamp, and put them in the mail.

6. Follow up with a phone call in one week.

The strategies, tactics, and plans you develop can be as broad or specific as your goals. To work in television is a specific goal. Therefore, your strategies, tactics, and plans are specific. If your goal is to be a 'star,' one strategy would be becoming a 'working actor.' Your tactic could be to generate exposure and create interest within the industry. Your plan would include training, acquiring the necessary marketing tools, and developing and implementing a sound marketing plan.

Organize yourself. Create a calendar with a daily 'to do' list.

EXAMPLE:

Monday:
Write and mail a personalized letter with a picture and resume to five targeted theatrical agents and managers.

Tuesday:

Write and mail a personalized letter with a picture and resume to five targeted commercial agents.

Wednesday:

Write and mail a personalized letter with a picture and resume to five targeted TV casting directors.

Thursday:

Write and mail a personalized letter with a picture and resume to five targeted feature casting directors.

Friday:

Write and mail a personalized letter with a picture and resume to five targeted commercial casting directors.

Follow-Up!

The following week, call those people to whom you mailed pictures. On Monday, call the five theatrical agents to whom you mailed your letters. Keep a notebook handy. Keep track of what you did and what was said in the phone call. If they say they are not interested, don't call back—but the following week, on Monday, write these same people again. Be persistent. Your intent is to get in the door.

"Actors should absolutely follow-up with mailings and phone calls once or twice to agents and managers, but not casting directors. If they say they're not interested, wait a while until you send or call an agent or manager again, or wait until you're in a show and then send them a flyer. You need to increase your 'market value,' to entice them to change their minds. I believe everyone can work if they have a strong enough will and sense of persistency."
Melisa Birnstein, manager
Associated Artists Management, L.A.
www.associatedartistsmngt.com

On Tuesday, Wednesday, and so forth, you will continue mailings and follow-up on the mailings from the week before. When making calls, be sure to get the names of those you speak with in the event you do not get through to the person whom you are trying to reach. Keep notes. When you call back, remembering the name of the person who answers the phone will be helpful in developing a rapport. He or she may be your best shot at getting through to the proper person.

Every other week you will choose five additional theatrical and commercial agents, five additional managers, and five additional TV, feature, and commercial casting directors to target.

Now, this does several things for you. It puts you in control of your career, which is very important. Knowing that you are getting up every day and doing something about your career will create a healthy, positive, and professional attitude.

This is just an example of how you might begin to organize yourself. Develop the system that works best for you. The most important thing is that you finish what you start.

"There is no point in time that an actor should stop sending his/her picture and resume if he/she is sending updates on his/her work. Who knows, one day through all of the persistency one of the companies just might say, 'all right already'."
Melisa Birnstein, manager
Associated Artists Management, L.A.
www.associatedartistsmngt.com

SCENE FIFTEEN
ARE U READY?

GOALS

Random House's definition of **goal** is, *"1. the result toward which effort is directed."* It is important to have both personal and professional goals. It is also important to have both **short-term** and **long-term goals**. You must define your goals, and develop a plan to achieve them. You must be flexible in your plan. Goals change, but only you can change them.

Personal Goals:

Your **personal goals** will influence and dictate certain **professional goals**. Begin with personal goals. Your personal goals, convictions, and morals, as well as who and what you are, will be the foundation of your business.

My Grandfather would often say, "Never do anything you wouldn't want to appear on the front page of the newspaper." It has always been a personal goal of mine to follow his words.

Here are a few examples of personal goals, as defined by some former students:

✔ "To have financial freedom"

✔ "To see the world"

✔ "To love what I do, and do what I love, for a living"

✔ "To be the **_best_** at whatever I do"

✔ "To acquire all the riches the world has to offer, as well as money and material possessions"

✔ "To provide my children with the same opportunities I have had"

A younger student's goal was:

✔ "To get good grades, a pony, and a new dress for Mom"

Your convictions, morals, who and what you are will influence many decisions you make in your career. Some actors who have strong religious beliefs will turn down roles that deal with issues like pre-marital sex, birth control and abortion. Other actors will turn down roles that involve nudity. There are actors that, for a variety of reasons, will turn down roles that glorify drug use and violence, and even roles that would require their character to smoke or drink.

Whatever your convictions may be, you must stick to them. Turning a role down is not easy, especially when you are starting out. When all is said and done, however, you will feel much better about yourself, your career and your business if you stick by your convictions.

Professional Goals:

Your *professional goals* are the goals, or *objectives*, of your business. It is vitally important to define the short and long-term goals of your business. I cannot stress this enough. It is particularly important when starting out. As you begin your career, the successes and failures of your business are based upon your achievement of goals. As your career progresses, you will be able to look at your career accomplishments and analyze industry feedback, as well. What is your ratio of callbacks to auditions? What is your ratio of bookings to auditions?

You must focus on your short and long-term goals, your objectives. For the purpose of this book, your long-term professional goal is to become a *working actor*. The long-term goal is easy. Short-term goals are more difficult. Definitive short-term goals, along with a time-line in which to achieve them, will help you gage your business's success and failure.

> *"Not everyone is going to have that 'career breaking role.' Most actors will find satisfaction in being a working actor. I'm not quite sure what that 'career breaking role' means anyway. Some actors like some singers may have that one 'breakout' song or performance and wind up in trivia or 'What Ever Happened To So and So' books."*
> **Al Onorato, manager**
> **Handprint Entertainment, L.A.**

Break your goals down into one-month, three-month, and six-month goals.

EXAMPLE:

One-Month Goals:

❏ Research and audit classes. *Begin training.*

❏ Research and interview photographers. *Have pictures taken.*

❏ *Create a professional resume.*

Three-Month Goals:

❏ *Create a data base.*

❏ Research and *target agents, managers, and casting directors.*

❏ Research and *compose cover letters.*

Six-Month Goals:

❏ *Obtain representation.*

❏ *Participate in an industry showcase.*

❏ *Go out on at least one audition.*

These are simplified examples. Your goals will be specific and much more detailed. You must create a time line for your goals. Identify the dates by which your goals must be accomplished. Use a calendar, or create a calendar on your computer, to chart your goals.

At the end of one month, three months, and six months, analyze your accomplishments. Did you meet your goals? Why weren't certain goals met? What have you done correctly? What have you done incorrectly? What do you need to do differently when you set your next goals?

Following clear-cut goals and objectives will also help you keep your business organized. Once you create a calendar of goals, you can then incorporate your mailings and follow-up dates. As you create your database, you will keep track of whom you meet, where and when you met them, and what you talked about. Incorporate your follow-up dates with these people in your calendar of goals.

Visualize!

When setting goals for yourself and your business, it is helpful to visualize yourself at the completion of specific goals. Goals are specific, detailed objectives. Desires are where you see yourself, or where you want to be. Close your eyes and see yourself cashing your first paycheck or watching yourself on TV. Visualize yourself where you want to be and imagine how you will feel when you get there. Use these images and feelings when times are tough or things just don't seem to be going your way.

It's Not for Me

It's not unusual for actors to relocate to New York or Los Angeles only to discover that this business is not for them. In the mean time, they have invested a great deal of money and time in acting classes, workshops, voice, dance, pictures, etc. The good news is, all of the time and money spent doesn't have to go to waste. If you decide this business is not for you, you can return home and enjoy the local acting scene.

There is always community theater, as well as local production companies that produce local TV and radio spots. Go ahead, be a 'big fish in a little pond.' Make that investment pay off. It's *okay* to be the local 'star.' You may even want to start giving your own acting classes to share your training and knowledge. And I might add, all the marketing information you're learning from this book can be applied in any market. If you've gone the formal route and earned a degree, you can teach acting in high school or college. I will always remember what my parents said to me when I left home and moved to New York. My Mother told me, "Remember, coming home is not a failure, it's just coming home." My Dad's farewell comment was, "I'm only a phone call away." He gave me a dime to hold onto. He has given me many dimes since.

REVIEW

Hopefully, you've read this book thoroughly—ideally, twice. You've taken detailed notes. You have acquired any additional reference material you need. You have completed your exercises and assignments, and have been keeping copious notes in your notebooks. If you haven't done everything you need to do, that's okay. **Take your time, and do it right.**

In the following chapter, you are going to assemble your marketing plan. You will be using all of the information you have researched, as well as all of your completed exercises and assignments.

Q & A

As you give this book a first read, it is important to look over the following questions, checklists, and marketing steps. Become familiar with the questions and terms. As you come across valuable information in your research, make mental notes. Do not attempt to assemble a marketing plan without the necessary research and tools. Again, take your time. Do it right. **This is your career. This is your business. This is your *future*.**

The following questionnaire will determine whether or not you're ready to assemble your marketing plan. Answer these questions in your notebook. Do not skip questions. There are bound to be some questions you can't answer. If this is the case, review your notes, exercises, assignments, and refer to the proper reference material.

PREPARING YOUR MARKETING PLAN

I. PRODUCT SUMMARY
A. How Do You Define Your Product?
1. What's your Type?
   a. Film Type?
   b. TV Type?
   c. Commercial Type?
2. Do you fit a Stereotype?
   a. Film Stereotype?
   b. TV Stereotype?
   c. Commercial Stereotype?

B. How Will You Refine Your Product?
1. Training?
   a. Technique Class?
   b. Audition Class?
      1. Film?
      2. Commercial
      3. Television? (Sitcom? Soap?)
   c. Workshops?
      1. Film?
      2. Commercial?
      3. TV/film?
      4. Scene Study?
      5. Improvisation?
   d. Voice/Diction Class?
      1. Voice-Over?
   e. Movement Class?
   f. Dialect Class?
2. Physical Refinement?
   a. Fitness?
   b. Complexion?
   c. Hair?
   d. Teeth?
   e. Contacts/Glasses?
3. What is your monthly budget for product refinement?
   a. Budget for training?
   b. Budget for physical refinement?

II. MARKET SUMMARY:
A. Do You Understand Your Market?
    1. What types of TV shows are popular and on the air now versus last season?
        a. Is there a pattern?
        b. Are they skewed toward younger or older audiences?
    2. What types, or genres of films are popular this year versus last year?
        a. Is there a pattern?
        b. Are they skewed towards younger or older audiences?
    3. Do you notice a pattern in commercials?

III. MARKET POSITIONING:
A. How do You Fit in the Market?
    1. What types of TV shows do you see yourself in?
    2. What types of films do you see yourself in?
    3. What types of commercials would best suit your type?

B. How Do You Compare with Your Competition?
    1. Are you comparably or better trained?
    2. Are you comparably or better skilled?
    3. Are you comparably or better fit?

IV. MARKETING OBJECTIVE:
A. What are Your Short-Term Goals?
    1. What do you need to accomplish?
        a. One-month goals?
        b. Three-month goals?
        c. Six-month goals?
    2. Where would you like to be?
        a. Three-month goals?
        b. Six-month goals?
        c. Nine-month goals?
    3. What happens if you fail to meet your goals?

B. What are Your Long-Term Goals?
    1. What do you need to accomplish?
        a. One-year goals?

      b. Ten-year goals?

      c. Career goals?

  2. Where would you like to be?

      a. One-year goals?

      b. Ten-year goals?

      c. Career goals?

  3. What happens if you fail to meet your goals?

C. What is Your Career Dream?

  1. In a perfect world, I would be (a)_____?

  2. In a perfect world, my yearly earnings would be _____?

  3. My role model is _____?

V. MARKETING TOOLS:

A. Do You Have Current and Professional Looking Pictures?

  1. If not, which photographer will you use?

  2. Who will you use for duplication?

      a. Lithograph?

      b. Photograph?

  3. Who will do your touch-ups?

  4. Will you have separate commercial and theatrical headshots?

  5. Will you be doing commercial print?

      a. Will you need a portfolio?

      b. Will you need Comp or Zed cards?

B. Do You Have Current and Professional Looking Resumes?

  1. Are they properly attached to your pictures?

C. Do You Have a Demo Reel?

  1. If so, is it professionally edited and packaged?

      a. Is it current?

      b. Will you need air-checks?

      c. Who will do your editing?

      d. Who will you use for dubbing?

      e. Which format; tape or CD-ROM?

D. Do You Have a Voice Demo?

  1. If so, is it professionally edited and packaged?

  2. Is it current?

E. Do You have a Separate Phone Line for Business?
    1. Does it have a reliable voice-mail feature?
    2. Can you check your messages remotely?

F. Do You Have a Wireless Phone or Pager?

G. Are You Maintaining a Database?
    1. Is your information current?

H. Do You Subscribe to any Breakdown Services?
    1. Which ones?

I. Do You Purchase or Subscribe to Industry Trades?
    1. Which ones?

J. Have You Purchased Your Industry Directories?
    1. Which ones?

K. Have you Selected and Prepared a Monologue?

L. What is Your Monthly Budget for Acquiring and Maintaining Current Marketing Tools?

VI. IMAGE AND PACKAGING:
A. Does Your Professional Image Project Your Type?
    1. Hair style?
    2. Clothing?
    3. Accessories?

B. Does Your Professional Image Reflect Your Age Range?
    1. Hair style?
    2. Clothing?
    3. Accessories?

C. Does Your Professional Image Reflect Your Camera Character?
    1. Hair style?
    2. Clothing?
    3. Accessories?

D. Are Your Personal and Professional Images Different?
1. Hair style?
2. Clothing?
3. Accessories?

E. Is it Difficult or Time Consuming to Re-Package Yourself?
From Your Personal to Professional Image?
1. Do you have an extreme hairstyle that you change?
2. Do you have noticeable piercing(s) that need to be taken out?
3. Do you wear extreme or stylized make-up that you change?
4. Do you have noticeable tattoos that need covering?
5. Do you wear extreme or stylized clothing?
   a. If so, do you have professional wardrobe as well?

VII. MARKET AWARENESS AND DEMAND:
A. How Will You Create Exposure for Your Product?
1. How often will you do industry showcases?
   a. When?
   b. Which ones?
2. Will you do theater?
   a. AEA waiver? Broadway? Off- or Off Off-Broadway?
   b. Dinner theater? Touring?
   c. Which ones?
3. Will you do experimental or student films?
   a. Who will you contact?
   b. How will you contact them?
4. Will you work as an extra?
   a. If so, which agencies will you register with?
5. How will you network with others in the industry?
6. Will you join any professional organizations?
   a. If so, which ones?
7. What is your monthly budget for product exposure?

B. What is Your Advertising Strategy?
1. What types of advertising mailings will you do?
   a. Targets?
   b. Schedule for mailings and follow-up?

2. Will you take advantage of casting directories? (optional)

3. What is your monthly budget for advertising?

C. What is Your Promotional Plan?
1. What is plan for promotional mailings?
   a. Targets?
   b. Schedule for mailings and follow-up?
2. Will you use any promotional products? (optional)
   a. If any, which types of promotional products will you use?
   b. If any, targets?
   c. If any, schedule?
3. Will you take advantage of internet casting services? (optional)
4. Will you create a website? (optional)
5. What is your monthly budget for product promotion?

D. What is Your Public Relations Strategy?
1. What is your plan for PR mailings?
   a. Targets?
   b. Schedule for mailings and follow-up?
2. When doing theater and showcases, how will you make use of industry comps?
   a. Targets?
3. What is your monthly PR budget?

VIII. FINANCING:
A. What Is Your Monthly Budget for Business Expenses?

B. What Is Your Monthly Budget For Personal Expenses?

C. How Will You Meet Your Budgetary Needs?
1. Day Job?
2. Savings?
3. Loans?

D. How Long Can You Survive Financially?

E. What Happens in the Event of Financial Troubles?

SCENE SIXTEEN
PLAN IMPLEMENTATION

MARKETING PLAN
Phase One

MARKETING TOOLS
PICTURES
- ❏ Research and Interview Photographers
- ❏ Select Photographer and Book Shoot Date
- ❏ Prepare for Photo Shoot
- ❏ Review Proofs and Select Head-shot
- ❏ Have any Lab Work Done and Have at Least 100 Theatrical and 100 Commercial Prints Made

RESUMES
- ❏ Create a Professional Resume
- ❏ Have at Least 200 Copies Made
- ❏ Correctly Attach Resume to Pictures

COMMUNICATION TOOLS
- ❏ Set-up a Dedicated Phone Line for Business
- ❏ Set-up Voice Mail
- ❏ Purchase a Pager or Wireless Phone
- ❏ Purchase or Have Access to a Fax Machine

REFERENCE MATERIAL
- ❏ Purchase or Subscribe to at Least One, Preferably Two Industry Trades
- ❏ Purchase Current Industry Directories
- ❏ Subscribe to a Breakdown Service (Optional)

ORGANIZATIONAL TOOLS
- ❏ Organize all Notes, Research, and Industry Contact Information
- ❏ Create Your Data Base

PRODUCT REFINEMENT
TRAINING
- ❑ Research Training Options
- ❑ Visit Schools and Audit Classes
- ❑ Enroll in at Least One Class and One Workshop (Start with technique)

PHYSICAL REFINEMENT
- ❑ Address Any Physical Issues You May Have (Consult a doctor when applicable)

MARKET AWARENESS AND DEMAND
ADVERTISING
- ❑ Organize Your Personalized Cover Letters, Pictures, and Resumes
- ❑ Purchase any Supplies Needed for Your First Mailing (Stamps, Envelopes, etc)
- ❑ Begin Your Mailing with Your Five Targeted Agents, Managers, and Casting Directors
- ❑ Create a Mailing Schedule to Keep Track of Mailing and Follow-up Dates

MARKETING PLAN
Phase Two

MARKET AWARENESS AND DEMAND
PRODUCT EXPOSURE
- ❏ Research, Audit, and Enroll in an Industry Showcase
- ❏ Research, Audit, and Enroll in a CD Workshop
- ❏ Explore any Theater Options (Optional, but great experience)
- ❏ Explore any Experimental or Student Film Options
- ❏ Register with an Extra Casting Agency (Work as an extra at least once for experience)
- ❏ Join or Form a Networking Group with Other Actors
- ❏ Consider Joining a Professional Organization

PROMOTIONAL PLAN
- ❏ Develop and Implement Your Plan for Promotional Mailings
- ❏ Consider the Use of Promotional Products (Optional)
- ❏ Create a Schedule to Keep Track of Mailing and Follow-up Dates

PUBLIC RELATIONS
- ❏ Develop a Plan For PR Mailings
- ❏ Use PR Mailings to Inform The Industry of any Product Exposure
- ❏ Use PR Mailings to Inform The Industry of any Change in Your Resume or Pictures.
- ❏ Use PR Mailings to Inform The Industry of any Change in Representation

ADVERTISING
- ❏ Follow-up on Your Mailing to Your Five Targeted Agents, Managers, and CDs
- ❏ Expand Your Mailing by Targeting an Additional Ten Agents, Managers, and CDs
- ❏ Place Your Headshot in the Players Directory
- ❏ Continue to Keep Track of Mailing and Follow-up Dates

PRODUCT REFINEMENT
TRAINING
- ❏ Continue to Research Training Options
- ❏ Continue to Visit Schools and Audit Classes
- ❏ If You are Not Working as an Actor, Continue Your Classes, Workshops, or Both.

ORGANIZATION
ADVERTISING

❑ Organize Your Personalized Cover Letters, Pictures, and Resumes
❑ Purchase any Supplies Needed for Your First Mailing (Stamps, Envelopes, etc)
❑ Begin Your Mailing with Your Five Targeted Agents, Managers, and Casting Directors
❑ Create a Mailing Schedule to Keep Track of Mailing and Follow-up Dates

APPENDIX A—WORKSHEETS

EXERCISE #1 WORKSHEET

HOW YOU PERCEIVE YOURSELF? TYPE? ROLE? AND WHY?
FILM:
TELEVISION:
COMMERCIALS:
EVERYDAY LIFE:

HOW DO YOUR FRIENDS PERCEIVE YOU?
1.
2.
3.
4.

HOW DO YOUR FAMILY MEMBERS PERCEIVE YOU?
1.
2.
3.
4.

HOW DO THOSE YOU DON'T KNOW PERCEIVE YOU?
1.
2.
3.
4.

EXERCISE #2 WORKSHEET

MAKE A LIST OF PROGRAMS THAT INTEREST YOU.

PROGRAM:
TEACHER(S):
ADDRESS:
PHONE:
WEB:
REFERRAL:
AUDIT DATE:
NOTES:

PROGRAM:
TEACHER(S):
ADDRESS:
PHONE:
WEB:
REFERRAL:
AUDIT DATE:
NOTES:

PROGRAM:
TEACHER(S):
ADDRESS:
PHONE:
WEB:
REFERRAL:
AUDIT DATE:
NOTES:

PROGRAM:
TEACHER(S):
ADDRESS:
PHONE:
WEB:
REFERRAL:
AUDIT DATE:
NOTES:

PROGRAM:
TEACHER(S):
ADDRESS:
PHONE:
WEB:
REFERRAL:
AUDIT DATE:
NOTES:

PROGRAM:
TEACHER(S):
ADDRESS:
PHONE:
WEB:
REFERRAL:
AUDIT DATE:
NOTES:

PROGRAM:
TEACHER(S):
ADDRESS:
PHONE:
WEB:
REFERRAL:
AUDIT DATE:
NOTES:

PROGRAM:
TEACHER(S):
ADDRESS:
PHONE:
WEB:
REFERRAL:
AUDIT DATE:
NOTES:

EXERCISE #3 WORKSHEET

Make a list of TV shows (sitcom, soaps and episodic), commercials and films that you see yourself on. (Observe the "types", the roles that you would play. Observe the way they dress, hairstyle, make-up, etc.)

	ROLE	STEREOTYPE	WARDROBE	HAIR/MAKE-UP

SOAPS:
1.
2.
3.
4.

SITCOM:
1.
2.
3.
4.

EPISODIC:
1.
2.
3.
4.

COMMERCIALS:
1.
2.
3.
4.

FILM:
1.
2.
3.
4.

EXERCISE #4 WORKSHEET

THEATRICAL AGENTS

THEATRICAL AGENT:
ASSISTANT(S):
AGENCY:
ADDRESS:
PHONE:
FAX:
WEB:
REFERRAL(?):

THEATRICAL AGENT:
ASSISTANT(S):
AGENCY:
ADDRESS:
PHONE:
FAX:
WEB:
REFERRAL(?):

THEATRICAL AGENT:
ASSISTANT(S):
AGENCY:
ADDRESS:
PHONE:
FAX:
WEB:
REFERRAL(?):

THEATRICAL AGENT:
ASSISTANT(S):
AGENCY:
ADDRESS:
PHONE:
FAX:
WEB:
REFERRAL(?):

THEATRICAL AGENT:
ASSISTANT(S):
AGENCY:
ADDRESS:
PHONE:
FAX:
WEB:
REFERRAL(?):

COMMERCIAL AGENTS

COMMERCIAL AGENT:
ASSISTANT(S):
AGENCY:
ADDRESS:
PHONE:
FAX:
WEB:
REFERRAL(?):

COMMERCIAL AGENT:
ASSISTANT(S):
AGENCY:
ADDRESS:
PHONE:
FAX:
WEB:
REFERRAL(?):

COMMERCIAL AGENT:
ASSISTANT(S):
AGENCY:
ADDRESS:
PHONE:
FAX:
WEB:
REFERRAL(?):

COMMERCIAL AGENT:
ASSISTANT(S):
AGENCY:
ADDRESS:
PHONE:
FAX:
WEB:
REFERRAL(?):

COMMERCIAL AGENT:
ASSISTANT(S):
AGENCY:
ADDRESS:
PHONE:
FAX:
WEB:
REFERRAL(?):

TALENT MANAGERS

TALENT MANAGER:
ASSISTANT (S):
COMPANY:
ADDRESS:
PHONE:
FAX:
WEB:
REFERRAL(?):

TALENT MANAGER:
ASSISTANT(S):
COMPANY:
ADDRESS:
PHONE:
FAX:
WEB:
REFERRAL(?):

TALENT MANAGER:
ASSISTANT(S):
COMPANY:
ADDRESS:
PHONE:
FAX:
WEB:
REFERRAL(?):

TALENT MANAGER:
ASSISTANT(S):
COMPANY:
ADDRESS:
PHONE:
FAX:
WEB:
REFERRAL(?):

TALENT MANAGER:
ASSISTANT(S):
COMPANY:
ADDRESS:
PHONE:
FAX:
WEB:
REFERRAL(?):

EXERCISE #5 WORKSHEET

THEATRICAL CASTING DIRECTORS

CASTING DIRECTOR:
ASSISTANT(S):
COMPANY:
ADDRESS:
PHONE:
FAX:
WEB:
REFERRAL(?):

CASTING DIRECTOR:
ASSISTANT(S):
COMPANY:
ADDRESS:
PHONE:
FAX:
WEB:
REFERRAL(?):

CASTING DIRECTOR:
ASSISTANT(S):
COMPANY:
ADDRESS:
PHONE:
FAX:
WEB:
REFERRAL(?):

CASTING DIRECTOR:
ASSISTANT(S):
COMPANY:
ADDRESS:
PHONE:
FAX:
WEB:
REFERRAL(?):

CASTING DIRECTOR:
ASSISTANT(S):
COMPANY:
ADDRESS:
PHONE:
FAX:
WEB:
REFERRAL(?):

COMMERCIAL CASTING DIRECTORS

CASTING DIRECTOR:
ASSISTANT(S):
COMPANY:
ADDRESS:
PHONE:
FAX:
WEB:
REFERRAL(?):

CASTING DIRECTOR:
ASSISTANT(S):
COMPANY:
ADDRESS:
PHONE:
FAX:
WEB:
REFERRAL(?):

CASTING DIRECTOR:
ASSISTANT(S):
COMPANY:
ADDRESS:
PHONE:
FAX:
WEB:
REFERRAL(?):

CASTING DIRECTOR:
ASSISTANT(S):
COMPANY:
ADDRESS:
PHONE:
FAX:
WEB:
REFERRAL(?):

CASTING DIRECTOR:
ASSISTANT(S):
COMPANY:
ADDRESS:
PHONE:
FAX:
WEB:
REFERRAL(?):

BACKGROUND CASTING AGENCIES/SERVICES

AGENCY:
ADDRESS:
PHONE:
FAX:
WEB:
REFERRAL(?):

AGENCY:
ADDRESS:
PHONE:
FAX:
WEB:
REFERRAL(?):

AGENCY:
ADDRESS:
PHONE:
FAX:
WEB:
REFERRAL(?):

APPENDIX B
RESOURCES AND INFORMATION

ACTING TEACHERS AND COACHES

LOS ANGELES

Carolyne Barry (Commercial)
323-654-2212
www.carolynebarry.com

Richard De Lancy
818-760-3110
www.delancy.com

Steve Eastin
Eastin Studio
818-980-9828
www.eastinstudio.com

Howard Fine
Howard Fine Studios
323-951-1221
www.howardfine.com

Diane Hardin
Young Actors Space
818-785-7979
www.young-actors-space.com

The Anita Jesse Studio
323-876-2870
www.anitajessestudio.com

Judy Kerr
818-505-9373
www.actingiseverything.com

Bobby Moresco
The Actors Gym
morescor@aol.com

Larry Moss
310 395-4284
www.fooledya.com

Susan Peretz Studios
323-852-0614

Brian Reise
323-874-5593

Stuart K. Robinson (Commercial)
310-558-4961

TJ Stein
Academy Training Center
818-771-8687

Stanzi Stokes
www.dwsactingstudio.com
818-762-8448

Carol Weiss (Musical Theater)
323-460-6006

NEW YORK

Jeff Barber
CTP Casting
800-234-5660
212-414-1930

William Esper
212-904-1350
www.esperstudio.com

Gene Frankel
212-777-1767
www.genefrankel.com

Uta Hagen
www.hbstudio.org

Wynn Handman
212-245-1271
www.americanplacetheatre.org

Olinda Turturro
212-473-1701
www.olindaturturroactingstudio.com

AIR CHECKS

LOS ANGELES
Jan's Video
323-462-5511
www.demo-reel.com
jansvideo@aol.com

Reel Video
323-466-5589
www.reelvideo.net

The Video Garage
310-441-9773

World of Video
310-659-5147
www.wova.com

NEW YORK
Dave's Air Checks
www.davesairchecks.com

Kenneth Garner
212-697-4420

CAREER CONSULTANTS

Jeff Barber
CTP Casting
800-234-5660
212-414-1930

Sam Christiansen
818-506-0783

Judy Kerr
818-505-9373
www.actingiseverything.com

Clair Sinnett
310-606-5626
866-4-ACTORS
www.actorsworking.com

Gerrie Wormser
310-277-3281

Gwyn Gississ
212-595-9001

CONSERVATORIES AND TRAINING

LOS ANGELES
American Academy of Dramatic Arts West
323-464-2777
www.aada.org

The Film Industry Workshops
818-769-4146

The Groundlings School
The Groundlings Theatre
213-934-4747
www.groundlings.com

Howard Fine Studio
323-951-1221
www.howardfine.com

The Lee Strasberg Theatre Institute
323-650-7777
www.strasberg.org

Playhouse West
818-881-6520
www.playhousewest.net

The Sanford Meisner Center for the Arts
818-769-5581
www.themeisnercenter.com

South Coast Repertory Conservatory
714-708-5500
www.scr.org

The Stella Adler Academy of Acting
323-465-4446
www.stellaadler-la.com

TVI Actors Studio
818-784-6500
www.tvistudios.com

NEW YORK
The Actors Center
212-447-6309
www.theactorscenter.org

The Acting Studio, Inc.
212-580-6600
www.actingstudio.com

The Actors Studio
212-757-0870
www.actors-studio.com

American Academy of Dramatic Arts
212-686-9244
www.aada.org

The American Place Theater
212-594-4482
www.americanplacetheatre.org

The Circle in the Square Theater School
212-307-0388
www.circlesquare.org

Creative Acting Company
212-352-2103
www.creativeacting.com

HB Studios
212-675-2370
www.hb-studios.com

The Lee Strasberg Theatre Institute
212-533-5500
www.strasberg.org

The Neighborhood Playhouse
212-688-3770
www.the-neiplay.org

The New Actors Workshop
212-947-1310
www.newactorsworkshop.com

The Stella Adler Conservatory
212-689-0087
www.stelladler.com

Ward Studio
212-239-1456
wardstudio@wardstudio.com

EQUITY WAIVER THEATERS

LOS ANGELES
Coast Playhouse
323-650-8509

Coronet Theater
310-657-7377

Court Theater
310-652-4035

Odyssey Theater
310-477-2055

Zephyr Theater
323-653-4667

NEW YORK
American Place Theater
212-594-4482

Arclight Theater
212-595-0355

Don't Tell Mama
212-757-0788

NY Theater Workshop
631-253-4715

Roundabout Theater
212-719-9393

EXTRA CASTING AGENCIES/SERVICES

LOS ANGELES
Cenex Casting (non-union)
www.entertainmentpartners.com
818-562-2799

Central Casting (union)
818-562-2700
www.entertainmentpartners.com

Bill Dance
www.billdancecasting.com
213-878-1131

Jeff Olan Casting (formerly Rainbow Casting)
818-752-2278
818-377-4475
www.jeffolan.com

NEW YORK
Background, Inc.
212-609-1103

The Casting Couch c/o CTP
212-696-1100

Extras by Booked
212-965-1683

Grant Wilfey Casting
212-686-3537

Liz Lewis Casting Partners
212-645-1500

Stark Naked Productions
(Elsie Stark Casting)
212-366-1903

Sylvia Fay Casting
212-889-2626

HOUSING

LOS ANGELES
Lakeside Apartments
Burbank: 818-845-8375

Laurel Apartments
LA: 323-656-1096

Oakwood Apartments
Burbank: 818-567-7368
LA: 310-448-4545

NEW YORK
The Actors' Fund of America
212-221-7300
www.actorsfund.org

The Gershwin Hotel
212-545-8000

Webster Apartments for Women
212-967-9000

PHOTO REPRODUCTION LABS

LOS ANGELES
Anderson Graphics
818-909-9100
310-278-9100
www.thevine.net

Isgo Lepejian
818-848-9001 - Burbank
323-876-8085 - Hollywood
www.isgophoto.com

Paragon Photo
323-933-5865
www.paragonphoto.com

Photo Max Lab
323-850-0200
www.photomaxlab.com

Prints Charm'n, Inc.
818-753-9055 - Studio City
310-288-1786 - West Hollywood
310-312-0904 - West Los Angeles
www.printscharmn.com

Producers & Quantity Photo Lab
213-462-1334
www.pqphoto.com

Ray the Retoucher
323-463-0555 - Hollywood
818-760-3656 - Studio City
818-841-9571 - Burbank
www.raytheretoucher.com

Reproductions
323-845-9595
www.reproductions.com

NEW YORK
Alluring Images
212-967-1610
www.alluringimages.com

Exact Photos
212-564-2568
800-536-3686

Ideal Photos of NYC
212-575-0303
800-929-5688
www.idealphotosofnyc.com

Modern Age
212-997-1800
212-279-1670
www.modernage.com

Precision Photos
212-302-2724
www.precisionphotos.com

Reproductions
212-967-2568
www.reproductions.com

PHOTOGRAPHERS

LOS ANGELES
Kevin McIntyre
310-212-4277
www.kevinmcphotograph.com

Bill Rich
310-207-0722
www.billrichphotography.com

Ron Sorensen
310-453-9116
714-642-8710, Costa Mesa
www.sorensonstudio.gobizgo.com

Dick Wieand
818-788-4746
www.isgophoto.com/wieand.html

Halstan Williams
310-393-3317
www.halstan.com

NEW YORK
Arthur Cohen
www.arthurcohen.com

Nick Granito
212-684-1056
www.nickgranito.com

David Morgan
212-989-3880

Phillip Stark Studio
212-868-5555
www.starkstudio.com

Richard Brinkoff Photography
212-620-7883

SHOWCASES: CD/AGENT

LOS ANGELES
AIA, Actor's Studio
818-563-4142
www.aiastudios.com

The Casting Break
818-783-8106
www.thecastingbreak.com

The Casting Network.com, Inc.
818-761-3103
www.thecastingnetwork.com

ITA Productions (formerly In The Act)
310/281-7772
www.itaproductions.com

Reel Pros
818-788-4133
www.reelpros.com

Sceneworks
818-761-3103

Steve Nave
818-763-6622

TVI
818-784-6500
www.tvistudios.com

NEW YORK
The Actor's Loft Lab
212-358-5003

Caroline Thomas' Total Theatre
212-799-4224
www.totaltheatrelab.com

Creative Acting Company
212-352-2103
www.creativeacting.com

T. Schreiber Studio
212-741-0209
www.t-s-s.org

TVI Actors Studio
212-302-1900
www.tvistudios.com

SHOWCASES: PREPARED SCENE

Prepared Scene showcases are usually with an acting director's class or workshop. When auditing a class or workshop, always ask if they offer a prepared scene showcase.

SPEECH AND DICTION COACHING

LOS ANGELES
Dudley Knight
949-856-2437
www.drama.arts.uci.edu

Robert Easton
818-985-2222
www.amath.colorado.edu/faculty/easton

Larry Moss
310-395-4284
www.foledya.com

NEW YORK
Catherine Fitzmaurice
The actors Center
212-447-6309

New York Speech Improvement Services
212-242-8435, appointment line
1-800-SPEAKWELL, tape orders
www.nyspeech.com

Amy Stoller
212-840-1234

TECHNIQUE TRAINING

LOS ANGELES

Bang Studio (improvisation)
323-653-6886
www.bangstudio.com

Brian Reise (cold read)
323-874-5593

Howard Fine Studio
323-951-1221
www.howardfine.com

Lee Strasberg Institute
323-650-7777
www.strasberg.org

The Sanford Meisner Center for the Arts
818-769-5581
www.themeisnercenter.com

Ned Manderino (Lee Strasberg)
323-650-7777

Playhouse West
818-881-6520
www.playhousewest.net

Ron Burrus (Stella Adler)
323-465-4446

Stella Adler Academy of Acting
323-465-4446
www.stellaadler-la.com

The Groundlings (improvisation)
323-934-4747
www.groundling.scom

Young Actors Space (youth)
818-785-7979
www.young-actors-space.com

NEW YORK

The Actors Studio
212-477-0171
www.actors-studio.com

HB Studios
212-594-4482
www.hb-studios.com

Neighborhood Playhouse
212-688-3770

Stella Adler Conservatory
212-689-0087
www.stellaadler.com

William Esper Studio
212-904-1350
www.esperstudio.com

UNIVERSITY PROGRAMS

American Conservatory Theatre (CA)
www.act-sfbay.org

American Film Institute (CA)
www.afi.com

Ball State University (IN)
www.bsu.edu

California Institute of the Arts
www.calarts.edu

Carnegie Mellon University (PA)
www.cmu.edu/cfa/drama

Columbia University (NY)
www.columbia.edu

Cranbrook Academy of Art (MI)
www.cranbrookart.edu/main.htm

The Julliard School (NY)
www.juilliard.edu/splash.html

The Actors Studio at The New School (NY)
www.newschool.edu/academic/drama

New York University
www.nyu.edu

North Carolina School of the Arts
www.ncarts.edu

Northwestern University (IL)
www.northwestern.edu

Rutgers – New Brunswick (NJ)
www.rutgers.edu

School of the Art Institute of Chicago (IL)
www.artic.edu

University of California-Irvine
www.uci.edu

University of California-Los Angeles
www.ucla.edu

University of California-San Diego
www.ucsd.edu

University of Southern California
www.usc.edu

University of Washington
www.washington.edu

Yale University (CT)
www.yale.edu

VIDEO DEMO EDITING
AND REPRODUCTION

Los Angeles:
Jan's Video
323-462-5511
www.videodemo.com

Reel Video
323-466-5589
www.reelvideo.net

World of Video
310-659-5147
www.wova.com

NEW YORK
Actor Demos
888-889-9009

Video Portfolios Productions, Inc.
800-725-0133
www.videoportfolios.com

VOICE-OVER CLASSES
AND DEMO PRODUCTION STUDIOS

LOS ANGELES
Carroll Voice Casting
213-851-9966
213-851-3973
www.voicetraxwest.com/casting.htm

Sandy Holt Voice Caster
310-271-8217

Kalmenson & Kalmenson Voice Casting
818-342-6499

Carole Wyand
ynotwyand@aol.com

NEW YORK
CPV Communications
www.cpvcom.com/contact.asp

One Destiny Productions, Inc.
212-629-6532
www.1destinyproductions.com

APPENDIX C
REFERENCE AND RECOMMENDED READING

AGENT DIRECTORIES

LOS ANGELES
AEA – Agent Listing
323-462-2334
www.actorsequity.org

Agencies/Keith Wolfe
310-276-9166
www.keithwolfe.com

The Agencies-
What Actors Need to Know/Lawrence Parke
800-379-5230
www.actingworldbooks.org

The Agency Guide – Breakdown Services
310-276-9166
www.breakdownservices.com

ATA – Agent Directory
310-274-0628
www.agentassociation.com

CSA – Agent Listing
323-463-1925
www.castingsociety.com

LA 411
323-965-2020
www.411publishing.com

Hollywood Creative Directory – Agents
www.hcdonline.com

Representation Directory
www.hcdonline.com

SAG (Screen Actors Guild) – Agent Listing
323-954-1600
www.sag.com

Working Actor's Guide to LA
310-965-0290
www.workingactors.com

NEW YORK
AEA NY – Agent Listing
212-869-8530
www.actorsequity.org

Agency Guide – Breakdown Services
212-869-2003
www.breakdownservices.com

CSA NY – Agent Listing
www.castingsociety.com

The New York Edition of Agencies
by Lawrence Parke
800-210-1197
www.actingworldbooks.org

Ross Report – TV/Film
www.rossreports.com

SAG NY - Agent Listing
800-205-7716
www.sag.com

CASTING DIRECTOR DIRECTORIES

LOS ANGELES
The Actor's Tool Box
www.theactorstoolbox.net

CD Directory – Breakdown Services
310-276-9166
www.breakdownservices.com

The Casting Directors by Keith Wolfe
323-469-5595
www.keithwolfe.com

Hollywood Creative Directory
323-308-3490
www.hcdonline.com

LA 411
323/965-2020
www.la411.com

The Working Actor's Guide to Los Angeles
310-965-0290
www.workingactors.com

NEW YORK
Henderson's Casting Directors Guide,
New York Edition
Sue Henderson
212-472-2292
www.hendersonenterprises.com

New York Casting Directory –
Breakdown Services
212-869-2003
www.breakdownservices.com

Ross Report
800/745-8922
www.rossreports.com

MANAGER DIRECTORIES

LOS ANGELES
Hollywood Creative Directory
323-308-3490
www.hcdonline.com

Personal Managers by Keith Wolfe
323-469-5595
www.keithwolfe.com

The Working Actor's Guide to L.A.
310-965-0290
www.workingactors.com

NEW YORK
Henderson's Personal Managers Directory
by Sue Henderson
212-472-2292
www.hendersonenterprises.com

PUBLICATIONS AND BOOK STORES

LOS ANGELES
Back Stage West
323-525-2356
www.backstagewest.com

The Hollywood Acting Coaches and Teachers
Directory by Lawrence Parke
800-379-5230
www.actingworldbooks.org

Hollywood Creative Directory
323-308-3490
www.hcdonline.com

The Hollywood Reporter
323-525-2000
www.hollywoodreporter.com

LA 411
323-965-2020
www.la411.com

Samuel French Theater and Film Bookshop
323-876-0570
www.samuelfrench.com

Take One Film and Theater Books
310-445-4050
www.take1filmbooks.com

Thomas Guide
800-899-6277
www.thomas.com

Variety
323-857-6600
www.variety.com

Where to Train by Keith Wolfe
323-469-5595
www.keithwolfe.com

The Working Actor's Guide to Los Angeles
310-965-0290
www.workingactors.com

NEW YORK
Backstage
212-536-5366
www.backstage.com

The Drama Bookshop
212-944-0595
www.dramabookshop.com

New York Public Library for the
Performing Arts
212-870-1630
www.nypl.org

Regional Theatre Directory
802-867-2223
www.theatredirectories.com
www.dorsettheatrefestival.org

Ross Report TV/Film
800-745-8922
www.rossreports.com

Showbusiness Weekly
212-986-4100
www.showbuisnessweekly.com

Theatre Communications Group
212-609-5900
www.tcg.org

RECOMMENDED READING

THE 9 STEPS TO FINANCIAL FREEDOM,
Suze Orman
THE ABC's OF SOAPS, Gwyn Gilliss

THE ART OF ACTING, Stella Adler
A DREAM OF PASSION, Lee Strasberg
ACTING IN FILM, Michael Caine
ACTING IS EVERYTHING, Judy Kerr
ACTING PROFESSIONALLY, Robert Cohen
AN ACTOR PREPARES,
Constantin Stanislavski
THE ARTIST'S WAY, Julia Cameron
AUDITION, Michael Shurtleff
BEING AND DARING, Eric Morris
BREAKING INTO COMMERCIALS,
Terry Berland and Deborah Ouellette
BUILDING A CHARACTER,
Constantin Staniskavski
THE DEVELOPMENT OF METHOD,
Lee Strasberg
*THE GREAT ACTING TEACHERS AND
THEIR METHODS*, Richard Brestoff
HITTING YOUR MARK, Steve Carlson
HOW TO BE A WORKING ACTOR,
Mari Lyn Henry and Lynne Rogers
HOW TO START ACTING IN FILM and TV,
Lawrence Parke
IMPROVISATION FOR THE THEATRE,
Viola Spolin
LET THE PART PLAY YOU, Anita Jesse
THE LONG SHMOOZE, Judy Belshe
ON ACTING, Sanford Meisner
RESPECT FOR ACTING, Uta Hagen
SECRETS OF SCREEN ACTING,
Patrick Tucker
TO THE ACTOR, Michael Chekhov
THE WORKING ACTOR,
Katinka Matson and Judith Katz
WORKING IN COMMERCIALS, Elaine
Keller-Beardsley

READING FOR PARENTS and MINORS (LA):

THE BLUE BOOK, THE EMPLOYMENT OF MINORS IN THE ENTERTAINMENT INDUSTRY, Studio Teachers – Local 884

IT'S A FREEWAY OUT THERE, THE PARENTS GUIDE TO THE FILM and *COMMERCIAL INDUSTRY,* Judy Belshe

THE MODELING HANDBOOK, Eve Matheson

SHOWBIZ KIDS HANDBOOK, TJ Stein
www.steinentertainmet.com

YOUR KID OUGHT TO BE IN PICTURES, Kelly Ford Kidwell and Ruth Devorin

WEB SITES AND INTERNET SERVICES

LOS ANGELES

The ActorSource
www.actorsource.com

Academy Players Directory
www.acadod.org

Academy of Motion Picture Arts and Sciences
www.oscars.org

Academy of Television Arts and Sciences
www.emmys.org

Actors Equity Association
www.actorsequity.com

Airline Travel. Car Rental. Hotel Reservations
www.travelocity.com

American Federation of Television and Radio Artists
www.aftra.org

Backstage West – LA
www.backstagewest.com

Breakdown Services
www.breakdownservices.com

The Casting Network
www.thecastingnetwork.com

The Cast List
www.thecastlist.com

Castnet
www.castnet.com

Consortium of Conservatory Programs
www.ncarts.edu/drama

Directors Guild of America
www.dga.org

Episodic Guide
www.epguides.com

ExtraCast
www.extracast.com

Free Scripts
www.script-o-rama.com

Film Search Tools
www.filmsite.org

Fox Searchlight
www.foxsearchlight.com

HollywoodAuditions.com
www.hollywoodauditions.com

The Hollywood Reporter
www.hollywoodreporter.com

Internet Movie Database
www.imdb.com

The Link
www.submitlink.com

Mapquest
www.mapquest.com

National Association of Schools of Theatre
www.arts-accredit.org

Playbill
www.playbill.com

Quiet Scream Publishing
www.quietscream.com

Samuel French Bookstore
www.samuelfrench.com

Screen Actors Guild
www.sag.org

Showfax
www.showfax.com

Showbiz. Ltd.
www.showbizltd.com

Showbusiness Weekly
www.showbusinessweekly.com

ShowMag.com
www.showmag.com

Stagebill
www.stagebill.com

TVI Studios
www.tvistudios.com

Variety
www.variety.com

Warner Brothers Studio Jobs
www.wbjobs.com

Writers Guild
www.wga.com

Xnet Information Systems
www.xnet.com

NEW YORK
Acting Zone Directory
www.actingzone.com/azdirectory

Actors Connection
www.actorsconnection.com

Actors Resource
www.actorsresource.biz/default.asp

Backstage – NY
www.backstage.com

Drama Bookshop
www.dramabookshops.com

NY Castings
www.nycastings.com

NY Players Guide
www.playersguideny.com

Manhattan Theatre Source
www.theatresource.org

Playbill
www.playbill.com

The Internet Theatre Database
www.theatredb.com

INDEX

Notes

Notes

Notes

Notes

Notes

CONTACT US

To arrange workshops and/or seminars at your school or organization,
please contact us at www.actorsworking.com or (866) 4-ACTORS.

To be notified of upcoming seminars and workshops,
send your name, address, phone number and email address to
Actors Working via fax at (310) 606-0823
or visit our website at www.actorsworking.com.

To arrange for a private coaching session in Los Angeles,
call (310) 606-5626.

For general information on Actors Working products and/or information
on licensing, domestic rights, authorization to photocopy items for corporate,
personal, or educational use, please call (866) 4-ACTORS.

For press review copies and/or author interviews and other publicity
information, please call (866) 4-ACTORS.

ACTORS WORKING
531 Main Street #1135
El Segundo, CA 90245
(866) 4-ACTORS
(310) 606-5626 off
(310) 606-0823 fax
www.actorsworking.com